Low-fat
family food

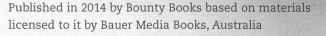

Published in 2014 by Bounty Books based on materials licensed to it by Bauer Media Books, Australia

Bauer Media Books are published by
Bauer Media Limited
54 Park St, Sydney; GPO Box 4088, Sydney,
NSW 2001, Australia.
phone (+61) 2 9282 8618; fax (+61) 2 9126 3702
www.awwcookbooks.com.au

MEDIA GROUP

BAUER MEDIA BOOKS

Publisher Jo Runciman
Editorial & food director Pamela Clark
Director of sales, marketing & rights Brian Cearnes
Creative director Hieu Chi Nguyen
Art director & designer Hannah Blackmore
Senior editor Wendy Bryant
Food concept director Sophia Young
Food editor Emma Braz

Printed by 1010 Printing Asia Limited in China.

Published and Distributed in the United Kingdom by
Bounty Books, a division of Octopus Publishing Group
Endeavour House
189 Shaftesbury Avenue
London WC2H 8JY
United Kingdom
phone (+44)(0)207 632 5400; fax (+44)(0)207 632 5405
info@octopus-publishing.co.uk;
www.octopusbooks.co.uk

International foreign language rights,
Brian Cearnes, Bauer Media Books
bcearnes@bauer-media.com.au

A catalogue record for this book is available from the British Library.

ISBN: 978-0-7537-2795-9

THE AUSTRALIAN
Women's Weekly

Low-fat
family food

Bounty
BOOKS

contents

Live life healthy

Many countries are experiencing an obesity epidemic with people of all ages facing bulging waistlines. The number of overweight people has increased steadily over the past 30 years. Being overweight results in an increased risk of developing life-threatening diseases such as type 2 diabetes, cardiovascular disease and high blood pressure.

Start healthy eating early

Low-fat family food is here to help start you and your family off on the right foot by encouraging healthy eating and an active lifestyle – after a few weeks of enjoying these tasty, and filling, low-fat recipes, you and your family will start to feel better. There is evidence that family meal patterns during childhood and adolescence affect diet and meal behaviour later in life. This book follows the *Australian Guide to Healthy Eating*, published by the Australian Government in 2012, which recommends that people consume a variety of foods across the five food groups and to avoid those that contain too much salt, sugar and saturated fat.

These recipes offer a wide variety of food from the five groups every day – lots of fruit and vegetables of different colours, legumes, grains, lean meats, fish, poultry, tofu and low-fat dairy products.

All the recipes include nutritional information and advice to help you adapt this healthy eating plan into a rewarding and sustainable lifestyle for you and your family.

Every family is different

You need to ensure the food your family is eating caters to everyone's age, health and energy levels. Children and teenagers are still growing, so they need sufficient foods to help with these increased nutritional requirements.

The book is full of helpful hints on how to adapt the recipes if you have particularly energetic family members who require additional kilojoules for energy.

Keep and stay active

Exercise is an integral part of a healthy lifestyle. Regular exercise reduces the risk of heart disease, diabetes and depression, and promotes a sense of wellbeing.

Make exercise part of an everyday routine – walk the dog, play in the backyard or the park, pop out for a walk at lunchtime. The earlier you start incorporating exercise as part of your family's daily life, the less it will feel like a chore.

Incidental exercise is all about the small amounts of exercise you perform during the day – taking the stairs instead of the lift, walking to the coffee shop, getting off the bus a stop earlier, even the housework – all of these help burn kilojoules.

Following the recipes in this book, and exercising regularly, will provide your family with the right tools to ensure a healthy lifestyle.

breakfast

The most important meal of the day, a good breakfast will stop you reaching for fat-filled snacks to curb hunger pangs.

breakfast
weekdays

bran and cranberry muesli

1 cup (90g) rolled oats

¾ cup (55g) All-Bran

¼ cup (35g) dried cranberries

1⅓ cups (330ml) skim milk

1 cup (150g) fresh blueberries

1 Combine oats, bran and cranberries in a small bowl to make muesli mixture.

2 Place ⅓ cup muesli in each bowl; top equally with milk and berries. Store remaining muesli in an airtight container.

prep time 5 minutes **serves** 4

tips If you don't want to use dried cranberries, use sultanas or raisins instead. The muesli recipe makes enough for 6 servings. If you don't feel like making some of the breakfasts we suggest, you can always have this muesli instead; remember, it's a ⅓ cup serving. You can always make a larger batch and keep it in an airtight container in the fridge.

To toast the oats, stir them in a heated small frying pan over medium heat until browned lightly; or roast them in the oven on an oven tray. Store the oats in a ziptop bag and sprinkle over the parfaits just before serving.

nutritional count per serving

- ▶ 1g total fat
- ▶ 0.2g saturated fat
- ▶ 664kJ (154 cal)
- ▶ 27.3g carbohydrate
- ▶ 7.2g protein
- ▶ 2g fibre

tip The parfaits can be made the night before and kept, covered, in the refrigerator. Layer the parfait with extra oats and extra cherries to increase the kilojoule count.

cherry parfait

2 tablespoons caster (superfine) sugar

⅓ cup (80ml) water

2 cups (300g) fresh or frozen seeded cherries, halved

1⅓ cups (380g) skim-milk yoghurt

2 teaspoons vanilla extract

pinch ground cinnamon

⅓ cup (30g) rolled oats, toasted

1 Combine sugar, the water and cherries in a medium saucepan; bring to the boil. Reduce heat; simmer, uncovered, about 2 minutes or until syrup thickens. Cool.

2 Meanwhile, combine yoghurt, vanilla and cinnamon in a small bowl.

3 Divide half the cherry mixture among four ¾-cup (180ml) glasses. Top with half the yoghurt, then remaining cherry mixture and yoghurt. Sprinkle with oats just before serving.

prep + cook time 20 minutes **serves** 4

nutritional count per serving

▶ 2.9g total fat   ▶ 43.3g carbohydrate
▶ 1.6g saturated fat   ▶ 7.7g protein
▶ 1013kJ (242 cal)   ▶ 5g fibre

ricotta and banana on toast

⅓ cup (80g) low-fat ricotta

4 slices rye bread (180g), toasted

4 small bananas (520g), sliced thickly

1 tablespoon honey

pinch ground cinnamon

1 Spread ricotta equally over toast slices; top with banana, drizzle with honey, then sprinkle with cinnamon.

prep time 5 minutes **serves** 4

tip Bananas can be swapped for poached or canned pears; this will increase your kilojoules by an extra quarter serve. Bananas are one of the best healthy snacks around; they are a good source of fibre, carbohydrate, and vitamin C, and are low in fat.

With its sweet taste, and because it's around 94% water, watermelon is a top diet food.

nutritional count per serving

▶ 0.9g total fat   ▶ 36.4g carbohydrate
▶ 0.2g saturated fat   ▶ 7.2g protein
▶ 828kJ (198 cal)   ▶ 5.5g fibre

watermelon, raspberry and cranberry salad

800g (1½ pounds) watermelon, cut into 2cm (¾-inch) pieces

2 cups (270g) fresh raspberries

1 cup (250ml) diet cranberry juice

2 tablespoons coarsely chopped fresh mint

1½ cups (300g) skim-milk fruit-flavoured yoghurt

1 Combine fruit, juice and mint in a medium bowl. Serve topped with yoghurt.

prep time 10 minutes   **serves** 4

tips Strawberries are a good, and cheaper, substitute for raspberries. Match the yoghurt flavour to your choice of berries. To increase your kilojoule intake, sprinkle 1 tablespoon of chopped pistachios over the watermelon; this will add an extra 293kJ (70 cal) to your daily intake.

nutritional count per 1 cup serving

▶ 1g total fat ▶ 30.9g carbohydrate
▶ 0.4g saturated fat ▶ 14.9g protein
▶ 830kJ (198 cal) ▶ 2.9g fibre

tips You can use ½ cup of fresh mixed berries and four ice-cubes instead of the frozen berries; garnish with extra fresh berries, if you like. You need 2½ Weet-Bix for the smoothie. Weet-Bix is a wheat-based breakfast cereal biscuit containing oven-roasted whole wheat grains, sugar, salt and barley malt extract. If you increase the serve to 1½ cups (375ml), this will add an extra 1245kJ (297 cal) to each serving.

high-fibre berry smoothie

2 cups (500ml) skim milk

½ cup (50g) crushed Weet-Bix

⅔ cup (190g) low-fat berry yoghurt

1 cup (150g) frozen mixed berries

1 Blend or process ingredients in two batches until smooth.

prep time 5 minutes **serves** 4

nutritional count per serving

▶ 4.5g total fat   ▶ 21.3g carbohydrate
▶ 1.4g saturated fat   ▶ 32g protein
▶ 1120kJ (267 cal)   ▶ 5.5g fibre

tips Cook the recipe just before serving. The frying pan goes under the grill in this recipe, so you need a frying pan with an ovenproof handle, or cover the handle with a few layers of foil to protect it from the heat of the grill. You could serve the omelette with two pieces of toast, this will add an extra 289kJ (69 cal) to each serving.

egg white omelettes with mushrooms

200g (6½ ounces) sliced ham off the bone

cooking-oil spray

200g (6½ ounces) button mushrooms, sliced thinly

12 egg whites

⅓ cup finely chopped fresh chives

2 medium tomatoes (380g), chopped coarsely

½ cup (60g) coarsely grated low-fat cheddar

4 slices wholemeal bread (180g), toasted

1 Discard any fat from ham; cut into thin strips. Lightly spray a 20cm (8-inch) (base measurement) non-stick frying pan with oil; cook ham, stirring, over medium heat, until browned lightly; remove from pan. Cover to keep warm.

2 Cook mushrooms in same heated pan, stirring, until browned lightly. Remove from pan; add to ham, cover to keep warm. Wipe pan clean.

3 Preheat grill (broiler).

4 Beat three of the egg whites in a small bowl with an electric mixer until soft peaks form; fold in 1 tablespoon of chives.

5 Lightly spray same heated pan with oil. Pour in egg-white mixture; cook, uncovered, over low heat, about 2 minutes or until just browned underneath. Sprinkle a quarter of the tomato over one half of the omelette. Top tomato with a quarter of the cheese. Place pan under hot grill; cook until top just sets and cheese melts. Top tomato with a quarter of the ham and a quarter of the mushroom; fold omelette in half to enclose filling. Carefully transfer omelette to a serving plate; cover to keep warm. Repeat to make another three omelettes.

6 Serve omelettes with toast, garnish with extra chives, if you like.

prep + cook time 25 minutes   **serves** 4

nutritional count per serving

▶ 2.4g total fat
▶ 0.4g saturated fat
▶ 1277kJ (305 cal)

▶ 62.7g carbohydrate
▶ 6.1g protein
▶ 8.5g fibre

porridge with apple compote

2 medium apples (300g)

½ teaspoon ground cinnamon

⅓ cup (80ml) water

8 dried apricots, halved

1 tablespoon sultanas

1 cup (90g) rolled oats

1 cup (250ml) skim milk

1½ cups (375ml) boiling water

1 tablespoon brown sugar

1 Peel, core and slice apple thickly. Place apple, cinnamon and the water in a medium saucepan; bring to the boil. Reduce heat, simmer, uncovered, for 2 minutes.

2 Add apricots and sultanas to pan; simmer, covered, about 5 minutes or until apple is tender.

3 Meanwhile, combine oats, milk and the boiling water in another medium saucepan; bring to the boil. Reduce heat, simmer, uncovered, stirring occasionally, about 5 minutes or until mixture thickens.

4 Serve porridge with compote; sprinkle with brown sugar.

prep + cook time 20 minutes **serves** 4

tip Any dried fruit, such as prunes, peaches or pears, could be used instead of the apricots.

The Australian Heart Foundation recommends adults eat around 25g-30g of fibre daily. This fibre-packed breakfast will get you off to a good start.

nutritional count per serving

▶ 26.6g total fat
▶ 9.7g saturated fat
▶ 1810kJ (433 cal)

▶ 27.7g carbohydrate
▶ 16.3g protein
▶ 9.1g fibre

breakfast burritos

250g (8 ounces) cherry tomatoes

2 teaspoons olive oil

420g (13½ ounces) canned kidney beans, rinsed, drained

⅓ cup coarsely chopped fresh flat-leaf parsley

1 tablespoon coarsely chopped pickled jalapeño chillies (optional, see tip)

1 tablespoon lime juice

1 large avocado (320g)

8 corn tortillas

50g (1½ ounces) baby spinach leaves

1 cup (120g) coarsely grated cheddar

1 Preheat grill (broiler).

2 Combine tomatoes and oil in a small shallow flameproof dish; grill about 15 minutes or until tomatoes have softened.

3 Combine beans, parsley, chilli and half the lime juice in a medium bowl with the tomatoes.

4 Mash avocado in a small bowl with remaining lime juice.

5 Warm tortillas according to packet directions. Top warmed tortillas with bean mixture, avocado, spinach and cheese.

prep + cook time 45 minutes **serves** 4

tips Jalapeño chillies are quite hot, omit them if serving to children, if you like. Flour or wholemeal tortillas can be used instead of the corn tortillas.

nutritional count per serving

- ▶ 2.8g total fat
- ▶ 0.5g saturated fat
- ▶ 1241kJ (297 cal)
- ▶ 43.3g carbohydrate
- ▶ 17.3g protein
- ▶ 13.4g fibre

tips Shortcut bacon is the largest, and leanest end of a bacon rasher. Any canned white beans can be used; we used cannellini beans in this recipe.

brekky beans

1 medium brown onion (150g), chopped finely

2 cloves garlic, crushed

4 shortcut bacon rashers (60g), chopped finely

800g (1½ pounds) canned diced tomatoes

2 tablespoons tomato paste

2 tablespoons wholegrain (seeded) mustard

800g (1½ pounds) canned white beans, rinsed, drained

⅓ cup coarsely chopped fresh flat-leaf parsley

4 slices rye bread (180g), toasted

1 Cook onion, garlic and bacon in a heated medium saucepan, over medium heat, for about 3 minutes or until onion softens.
2 Add tomatoes, paste and mustard; cook, stirring, about 5 minutes or until hot. Add beans; cook, stirring, until heated through. Remove from heat; stir in parsley.
3 Serve bean mixture with toast.

prep + cook time 20 minutes **serves** 4

serving suggestion Serve with an extra piece of toast; this will add an extra 289kJ (69 cal) to each serving.

healthy snacks

fruit nibble mix

Break 3 rosemary and sea salt grissini into small pieces into a medium bowl; add 30g (1 ounce) puffed corn, ¼ cup quartered dried apricots, ¼ cup coarsely chopped dried pears and ¼ cup coarsely chopped seeded dried dates, mix well. Serve ⅓ cup nibble mix in each bowl. Store remaining nibble mix in an airtight container for use on other days.

prep time 10 minutes **makes** 2⅔ cups
nutritional count per ⅓ cup serving 0.1g total fat (0g saturated fat); 217kJ (52 cal); 11.7g carbohydrate; 0.7g protein; 1.4g fibre

tip Grissini are crisp, thin breadsticks and are available in a variety of flavours, in packets, from most large supermarkets; use any flavour you like.

cinnamon crisps

Preheat oven to 180°C/350°F. Line an oven tray with baking paper. Spray 2 rye mountain bread wraps with oil. Sift 1 tablespoon icing (confectioners') sugar and ½ teaspoon ground cinnamon over wraps. Cut wraps in half crossways; cut each half into wide strips. Place on oven tray; bake about 4 minutes or until crisp. Cool on trays.

prep + cook time 10 minutes **serves** 4
nutritional count per serving 0.8g total fat (0.1g saturated fat); 230kJ (55 cal); 10.4g carbohydrate; 1.4g protein; 0.6g fibre

tip Store crisps in an airtight container for up to 5 days.

seeded mustard crisps

Preheat oven to 180°C/350°F. Line oven tray with baking paper. Spray 2 rye mountain bread wraps with oil; spread with 1 tablespoon dijon mustard, then sprinkle with 2 teaspoons poppy seeds, 1 teaspoon sweet paprika and ½ teaspoon sea salt flakes. Cut wraps in half crossways; cut each half into long thin triangles. Place triangles on tray; bake about 4 minutes or until crisp. Cool on trays.

prep + cook time 20 minutes **serves** 4
nutritional count per serving 1.2g total fat (0.2g saturated fat); 201kJ (48 cal); 6.6g carbohydrate; 1.5g protein; 0.9g fibre

tip Store crisps in an airtight container for up to 5 days.

spiced popcorn

Place 2 tablespoons popping corn in an oven bag or paper bag; secure loosely with kitchen string. Microwave bag on MEDIUM-HIGH (75%) for about 4 minutes or until popped. Carefully remove bag from microwave with tongs; stand for 2 minutes before opening. Meanwhile, dry-fry 1 teaspoon each of ground coriander and cumin and ½ teaspoon ground cinnamon in a heated small frying pan until fragrant. Break 30g (1 ounce) mini plain pappadums into pieces into a medium bowl; add popcorn and spices, toss gently to combine.

prep + cook time 10 minutes **serves** 4
nutritional count per serving 1.1g total fat (0.3g saturated fat); 184kJ (44 cal); 5.5g carbohydrate; 2g protein; 1.8g fibre

tip Store popcorn in an airtight container for up to 3 days.

breakfast weekends

breakfast fry-up

2 small tomatoes (180g), quartered

1 tablespoon balsamic vinegar

150g (4½ ounces) mushrooms, sliced thickly

100g (3 ounces) baby spinach leaves

2 tablespoons coarsely chopped fresh basil

2 slices rye bread (90g), toasted

1 Preheat oven to 220°C/425°F.

2 Combine tomato and half the vinegar in a small shallow baking dish. Roast, uncovered, about 10 minutes.

3 Meanwhile, cook mushrooms, spinach and remaining vinegar in a large frying pan, over medium heat, until mushroom is tender and spinach wilts; stir in basil.

4 Serve tomato and mushroom mixture on toast.

prep + cook time 15 minutes **serves** 4

tips It's worth buying the best, most flavoursome tomatoes you can. We used a balsamic vinegar bought from the supermarket, but if you're lucky enough to have a first-grade balsamic vinegar, use it sparingly, as you might only need 1 teaspoon instead of 1 tablespoon. You could add some pan-fried bacon or prosciutto, if you like. Two slices would add 439kJ (105 cal) to each serve.

nutritional count per serving

▶ 1.5g total fat ▶ 22.5g carbohydrate
▶ 0.1g saturated fat ▶ 8.9g protein
▶ 652kJ (156 cal) ▶ 7.6g fibre

The cottage cheese can be substituted with low-fat ricotta, if you like.

nutritional count per serving

▶ 6.1g total fat ▶ 50.4g carbohydrate
▶ 1.4g saturated fat ▶ 19.3g protein
▶ 1476kJ (353 cal) ▶ 8.4g fibre

corn fritters

2 eggs

620g (1¼ ounces) canned corn kernels, rinsed, drained

1 small red onion (100g), sliced thinly

1 cup (160g) wholemeal self-raising flour

⅔ cup (160ml) skim milk

cooking-oil spray

⅔ cup (130g) low-fat cottage cheese

1 Whisk eggs in a medium bowl; stir in corn, onion, flour and milk.

2 Spray a large frying pan with oil. Pour ⅓-cups of batter into heated pan; cook, over medium heat, about 2 minutes or until bubbles appear. Turn fritters; cook until lightly browned on the other side. Repeat with remaining mixture.

3 Serve warm fritters dolloped with cheese; sprinkle with fresh dill or parsley, if you like.

prep + cook time 20 minutes **serves** 4

tip If you'd rather cook fresh corn, the easiest way is to coat the cob lightly with cooking-oil spray, then cook it on the barbecue or on a grill pan, turning the cob until it's lightly charred all over. Place the cob on a board and slice off the kernels.

Any berries in season can be substituted for those used here. The strawberries, raspberries and orange juice means this breakfast favourite is full of vitamin C.

tip The berry compote can be made the day before; store, covered, in the fridge.

crumpet with berry compote

1 cup (150g) self-raising flour

¼ teaspoon fine salt

¼ teaspoon caster (superfine) sugar

¾ cup (180ml) warm water

¼ teaspoon instant yeast

cooking-oil spray

berry compote

125g (4 ounces) strawberries, quartered

125g (4 ounces) blueberries

150g (4½ ounces) raspberries

1 teaspoon finely grated orange rind

¼ cup (60ml) orange juice

2 tablespoons icing (confectioners') sugar

1 Make berry compote.

2 Meanwhile, sift flour, salt and sugar into a medium bowl.

3 Combine the water and yeast in a small heatproof jug; add yeast mixture to flour mixture, stir until smooth.

4 Place four egg rings in a heated oiled large frying pan; lightly spray each ring with oil. Fill each ring three-quarters full with crumpet mixture. Cook crumpets, over low heat, for about 10 minutes or until surface is covered with burst air bubbles. Remove rings from crumpets, cover pan; cook crumpets a further 3 minutes or until the surface is firm. Remove from pan; cool on a wire rack. Repeat with the remaining mixture to make a total of 8 crumpets.

5 To serve, toast crumpets; top with berry compote. Dust with extra sifted icing sugar, if you like.

berry compote Combine ingredients in a medium bowl. Cover; refrigerate 1 hour.

prep + cook time 1 hour (+ refrigeration) **serves** 4

tips You can warm the tortillas in the microwave oven; follow the directions on the packet. We used a mixture of baby heirloom tomatoes, available from most larger supermarkets. Omit the chilli if you like.

chunky mexican-style salsa with tortillas

1 medium red onion (180g), cut into thin wedges

pinch dried chilli flakes

800g (1½ pounds) mixed baby tomatoes, halved

2 medium red capsicums (bell pepper) (400g), chopped coarsely

⅓ cup (80ml) water

2 tablespoons balsamic vinegar

4 small white corn tortillas (110g)

⅓ cup firmly packed fresh coriander leaves (cilantro)

⅓ cup firmly packed fresh flat-leaf parsley leaves

1 Heat a lightly oiled non-stick frying pan over medium heat; cook onion and chilli, stirring, until onion softens. Add tomato, capsicum, the water and vinegar; bring to the boil. Reduce heat; simmer, uncovered, stirring occasionally, about 15 minutes or until capsicum is tender and tomato begins to soften. Season to taste.

2 Meanwhile, cook tortillas, one at a time, in a heated small frying pan over high heat, about 1 minute each side or until browned lightly and warmed through.

3 Serve tomato mixture with tortillas; sprinkle with coriander and parsley.

prep + cook time 25 minutes **serves** 4

serving suggestion You could add a small avocado to the salsa; this will increase each serve by 301kJ (72 cal).

tips Cook pancakes just before serving. Pears can be made a day ahead; thicken syrup just before serving.

buttermilk pancakes with golden pears

1 cup (150g) self-raising flour

1 cup (250ml) buttermilk

2 egg whites

cooking-oil spray

golden pears

4 corella pears (400g), peeled, halved, cored

¼ cup (90g) golden syrup

2 cups (500ml) water

1 tablespoon lemon juice

1 teaspoon cornflour (cornstarch)

1 tablespoon water, extra

1 Make golden pears.

2 Sift flour into a small bowl; gradually whisk in combined buttermilk and egg whites to make a smooth batter.

3 Lightly spray a heated large non-stick frying pan. Pour ¼ cup batter into pan; use the back of a spoon to spread the batter into a 10cm (4-inch) round shape. Cook, over low heat, about 2 minutes or until bubbles appear on the surface. Turn pancake; cook until browned lightly on the other side. Remove from pan; cover to keep warm. Repeat with remaining batter to make a total of 8 pancakes. Serve with pears and syrup.

golden pears Place pears in a small saucepan with syrup, the water and juice; bring to the boil. Reduce heat, simmer, uncovered, turning occasionally, about 15 minutes or until pears are just tender. Remove pears from syrup; reserve syrup. Stir the blended cornflour and the extra water into reserved syrup; stir over heat until the mixture boils and thickens.

prep + cook time 35 minutes **serves** 4

nutritional count per serving

▶ 9.8g total fat   ▶ 5.1g carbohydrate
▶ 4.6g saturated fat   ▶ 12.2g protein
▶ 686kJ (164 cal)   ▶ 3.4g fibre

tip You can make these in a standard muffin pan, if you like; line the holes with paper cases, or a folded square of baking paper, as we did here.

baked ricottas with roasted tomatoes

cooking-oil spray

1 tablespoon pine nuts

2 cloves garlic, crushed

140g (4½ ounces) baby spinach leaves

1⅓ cups (320g) low-fat ricotta

2 egg whites, beaten lightly

2 tablespoons coarsely chopped fresh chives

500g (1 pound) baby truss tomatoes

1 tablespoon balsamic vinegar

1 Preheat oven to 220°C/425°F. Lightly spray 4 x ⅓-cup (80ml) ramekins with oil.

2 Heat a large non-stick frying pan over low heat; cook nuts and garlic, stirring, until fragrant. Add spinach, stir until wilted. Cool mixture 10 minutes.

3 Combine ricotta, egg white and chives in a medium bowl with spinach mixture; divide the mixture into ramekins.

4 Bake, uncovered, about 20 minutes or until ricotta is browned lightly.

5 Meanwhile, toss tomatoes with vinegar; place on an oven tray. Roast, uncovered, for 10 minutes or until softened. Serve baked ricottas with roasted tomatoes.

prep + cook time 40 minutes **serves** 4

serving suggestion Serve ricotta with two thin slices of toasted ciabatta; this will add 659kJ (157 cal) to each serve.

Antioxidants help to prevent cell damage, and capsicum and zucchini are full of them.

tips The vegetables can be cooked the night before; store them, covered, in the refrigerator. Toast the bread just before serving.

grilled vegetables with ricotta

2 medium zucchini (240g), sliced thinly lengthways

2 medium yellow capsicums (bell pepper) (400g), sliced thickly

2 medium tomatoes (300g), halved

4 slices ciabatta bread (140g)

cooking-oil spray

2 tablespoons low-fat ricotta

2 tablespoons small fresh basil leaves

60g (2 ounce) baby rocket leaves (arugula)

1 Lightly spray zucchini, capsicum, tomato and bread with oil; season vegetables. Cook vegetables and bread, in batches, on a heated grill plate (or grill or barbecue) until vegetables are tender and bread is browned lightly.

2 Spread cheese over toast slices; sprinkle with basil. Serve with vegetables and rocket.

prep + cook time 30 minutes **serves** 4

serving suggestion Serve with a poached egg; this will add an extra 309kJ (74 cal) to each serve.

tips If your frying pan does not have a heatproof handle, cover the handle with a couple of layers of aluminium foil to protect it from the heat of the grill. Serve frittata with one piece of grilled ciabatta; this will add 329kJ (79 cal) to each serve.

asparagus frittata with rocket salad

cooking-oil spray

1 medium red onion (180g), sliced thinly

340g (11 ounces) asparagus, trimmed, cut into 2cm (¾-inch) lengths

4 eggs

4 egg whites

⅓ cup (65g) low-fat cottage cheese

80g (2½ ounces) baby rocket leaves (arugula)

⅓ cup (80ml) lemon juice

1 tablespoon rinsed, drained baby capers

1 Preheat grill (broiler).

2 Lightly spray a large frying pan with oil; cook onion over medium heat, stirring, for 1 minute. Add asparagus; cook, stirring, 2 minutes.

3 Meanwhile, combine eggs, egg whites and cheese in a medium jug. Pour over asparagus mixture in pan. Cook, uncovered, over medium heat, for about 5 minutes or until frittata is browned underneath.

4 Place pan under grill for about 5 minutes or until frittata is set.

5 Combine remaining ingredients in a medium bowl; serve frittata with salad.

prep + cook time 25 minutes **serves** 4

Frittata is delicious warm, but if you want to take it to work, keep it in the fridge, then wrap it in plastic the next morning.

Salmon is a good source of vitamin D
(essential for good bone health),
which is vital as we age to keep us
steady and on our feet.

smoked salmon and poached egg on rye

4 eggs

170g (5½ ounces) asparagus, halved crossways

4 slices rye bread (180g), toasted

200g (6½ ounces) smoked salmon

2 tablespoons fresh chervil leaves

1 Half fill a large shallow frying pan with water; bring to the boil. Break one egg into a cup, then slide it into the pan. When all the eggs are in the pan, allow water to return to the boil.

2 Cover pan, turn off heat; stand eggs about 3 minutes or until a light film sets over the egg yolks. Remove eggs, one at a time, using a slotted spoon; place spoon on kitchen paper briefly to blot up poaching liquid.

3 Meanwhile, boil, steam or microwave asparagus until just tender; drain.

4 Divide toast among serving plates; top each with salmon, egg then asparagus; sprinkle with chervil to serve.

prep + cook time 10 minutes **serves** 4

tips Swap chervil for dill or parsley, if you like. Smoked salmon can be swapped for prosciutto.

nutritional count per serving

▸ 0.2g total fat
▸ 0.1g saturated fat
▸ 213kJ (51 cal)
▸ 8.2g carbohydrate
▸ 4.9g protein
▸ 1.9g fibre

nutritional count per serving

▸ 0.5g total fat
▸ 0g saturated fat
▸ 138kJ (33 cal)
▸ 9.6g carbohydrate
▸ 1.1g protein
▸ 3.6g fibre

healthy drinks

melon & berry frappe

Blend 800g (1½ pounds) coarsely chopped seedless watermelon, 1⅓ cups frozen raspberries, 2 teaspoons finely grated lime rind, ¼ cup lime juice and 24 ice cubes until mixture is smooth.

prep time 10 minutes **serves** 4
tip Use any melon and berry combination; just ensure you use the same amount as specified in the recipe.

pine berry lassi

Blend 1 cup skim milk, ⅓ cup skim-milk yoghurt, 200g (6½ ounces) coarsely chopped fresh pineapple, 250g (8 ounces) halved strawberries and 24 ice cubes until smooth.

prep time 10 minutes **serves** 4
tip Vary the fruit according to your taste and what's in season; just ensure you use the same amount as specified in the recipe.

nutritional count per serving

▸ 0.3g total fat
▸ 0g saturated fat
▸ 451kJ (108 cal)

▸ 24.3g carbohydrate
▸ 2.2g protein
▸ 5.1g fibre

nutritional count per serving

▸ 0.4g total fat
▸ 0g saturated fat
▸ 598kJ (143 cal)

▸ 34.7g carbohydrate
▸ 1.4g protein
▸ 7g fibre

peach, apple & berry juice

Push 4 coarsely chopped medium apples, 1 coarsely chopped medium peach and 8 strawberries through a juice extractor into a large jug; stir to combine.

prep time 10 minutes **serves** 4
tip We used green apples in this recipe, but you can use the colour of your choice.

apple & celery juice

Push 5 coarsely chopped large apples and 4 trimmed coarsely chopped celery stalks through a juice extractor into a large jug; stir to combine.

prep time 10 minutes **serves** 4
tip We used green apples in this recipe, but you can use the colour of your choice.

lunch

Stop calorie-laden afternoon munchies with a healthy and filling lunch. Most of these are suitable for work and school.

lunch
weekdays

turkey vietnamese roll

1 large carrot (220g)

2 lebanese cucumbers (130g)

4 green onions (scallions)

4 small torpedo-shaped white bread rolls (340g)

1 tablespoon low-fat mayonnaise

100g (3 ounces) shaved smoked turkey breast

½ cup fresh coriander leaves (cilantro)

1 fresh small red thai (serrano) chilli, sliced thinly

1 tablespoon light soy sauce

1 Using a vegetable peeler, cut long thin strips from the carrot and cucumbers. Thinly slice onions lengthways.
2 Split bread rolls lengthways through top, without cutting all the way through.
3 Spread inside of each roll with 1 teaspoon mayonnaise; top equally with carrot, cucumber, onion, turkey, coriander and chilli; drizzle with the sauce.

prep time 10 minutes **serves** 4

tips The turkey can be swapped for cooked chicken breast. Vegetables can be prepared a day ahead, cover with damp kitchen paper and plastic wrap, and store in the fridge. Drizzle with soy sauce just before serving.

nutritional count per serving

▶ 6g total fat
▶ 1.3g saturated fat
▶ 1330kJ (318 cal)

▶ 48g carbohydrate
▶ 13.5g protein
▶ 8g fibre

You can add or omit the chilli depending on how hot you like your food.

We used a mixture of parsley, basil and dill for this recipe, but you can use any herbs you like.

nutritional count per serving

▶ 5.3g total fat   ▶ 14.1g carbohydrate
▶ 1.9g saturated fat   ▶ 19.4g protein
▶ 805kJ (192 cal)   ▶ 4.2g fibre

tips If your frying pan does not have a heatproof handle, cover the handle with a couple of layers of aluminium foil to protect it from the heat of the grill. The frittata can be served warm or cold. Reheat slices, covered, in a microwave oven on HIGH (100%) for about 1 minute.

primavera frittata

1 medium brown onion (150g), chopped finely

1 clove garlic, crushed

1 large potato (300g), trimmed, chopped coarsely

170g (5½ ounces) asparagus, chopped coarsely

1 medium zucchini (120g), sliced thinly

3 eggs

9 egg whites

⅓ cup (80ml) skim milk

¼ cup finely chopped fresh herbs (see tip, left)

⅓ cup (40g) frozen peas

2 tablespoons finely grated parmesan

1 tablespoon fresh dill sprigs

1 Heat a medium (22cm/9-inch base) non-stick frying pan over medium heat; cook onion and garlic, stirring, about 10 minutes or until onion is browned lightly.

2 Meanwhile, boil, steam or microwave potato, asparagus and zucchini, separately, until tender; drain.

3 Whisk eggs, egg whites, milk and herbs in a large jug; season.

4 Add potato, asparagus and zucchini to onion mixture in pan. Pour egg mixture over vegetables; sprinkle with peas. Reduce heat to low; cook, uncovered, about 10 minutes or until frittata is almost set. Sprinkle with cheese.

5 Preheat grill (broiler). Grill frittata about 3 minutes or until set. Stand frittata in the pan for 5 minutes before sprinkling with dill and serving.

prep + cook time 35 minutes   **serves** 4

tips You could use short-grain or brown rice instead of the sushi rice. Add some pickled ginger, if you like. The salad can be made a day ahead; store, covered, in the fridge. This is a good recipe for a work lunch.

teriyaki chicken rice salad

1 cup (200g) sushi rice

1½ cups (375ml) water

¼ cup (60ml) rice vinegar

¼ cup (60ml) teriyaki sauce

4cm (1½-inch) piece fresh ginger (20g), grated

2 cups (320g) shredded skinless cooked chicken

2 lebanese cucumbers (260g), seeded, chopped finely

2 medium carrots (240g), cut into matchsticks

120g (4 ounces) baby spinach leaves

1 tablespoon sesame seeds, toasted

1 sheet toasted seaweed (yaki-nori), shredded finely

1 Rinse rice under cold water until water runs clear; drain.
2 Combine rice and the water in a small saucepan, cover; bring to the boil. Reduce heat; simmer, covered, about 10 minutes or until rice is tender. Remove from heat; stand, covered, until cold.
3 Combine rice with vinegar, sauce and ginger in a large bowl. Add chicken, cucumber, carrot, spinach and seeds; toss gently to combine. Season to taste. Serve rice salad sprinkled with nori.

prep + cook time 35 minutes (+ standing)   **serves** 4

Prick the potatoes all over with a fork if you're cooking them in a microwave oven, otherwise they'll explode.

potato, tuna and egg salad

You need four hard-boiled eggs for this recipe.

12 baby new potatoes (480g)

200g (6½ ounces) green beans, trimmed, halved crossways

⅓ cup (95g) skim-milk natural yoghurt

2 teaspoons finely grated lemon rind

2 teaspoons lemon juice

420g (13½ ounces) canned tuna in springwater, drained, flaked

6 green onions (scallions), sliced finely

2 tablespoons coarsely chopped fresh flat-leaf parsley

4 hard-boiled eggs, quartered

1 Boil, steam or microwave potatoes and beans, separately, until tender; drain, cool.

2 Meanwhile, make dressing by combining yoghurt, rind and juice in a medium bowl.

3 Quarter potatoes; add to dressing with tuna, onion, beans and parsley, stir to combine. Serve salad topped with egg.

prep + cook time 15 minutes **serves** 4

tips The salad can be made the night before; store, covered, in the fridge. To make the perfect hard-boiled eggs, place eggs in a small saucepan and cover with cold water. Bring to the boil; boil, uncovered, for 3½ minutes, drain. Shell eggs when cool enough to handle.

tips Keep the rolls moist by covering them with a slightly damp piece of kitchen paper, then store them in an airtight container in the fridge. Rolls can be made a day ahead. Swap the tofu for cooked shredded chicken breast for a non-vegetarian option.

shredded vegetable rice paper rolls

1 medium red onion (170g), sliced thinly

2 large yellow capsicums (bell pepper) (700g), sliced thinly

300g (9½ ounces) snow peas, trimmed, sliced thinly

3 cups (240g) finely shredded wombok (napa cabbage)

2 large carrots (360g), grated coarsely

100g (3 ounces) rice vermicelli

2 lebanese cucumbers (260g), cut into matchsticks

⅔ cup each loosely packed fresh mint and coriander leaves (cilantro)

12 x 22cm (9-inch) rice paper rounds

400g (12½-ounce) piece marinated tofu, cut into 6 slices, then halved lengthways

1 cup (250ml) sweet chilli sauce

1 Combine onion, capsicum, snow peas, wombok and carrot in a medium bowl; cook wombok mixture in a heated large non-stick frying pan, over medium heat, stirring, about 5 minutes or until vegetables soften. Strain mixture into a colander over a large bowl; stand until cool.

2 Meanwhile, place vermicelli in a small heatproof bowl, cover with boiling water; stand until tender, drain. Using kitchen scissors, cut vermicelli coarsely.

3 Combine vegetable mixture and vermicelli in a medium bowl with cucumber and herbs; season.

4 Dip one rice paper round into a bowl of warm water until soft. Lift sheet from water; place on a clean tea towel. Top with one heaped tablespoon of vegetable mixture and one slice of tofu; drizzle with a little of the sauce. Fold sheet over filling, then fold in both sides. Continue rolling to enclose filling.

5 Repeat step 4 to make a total of 12 rolls. Serve rolls with remaining sauce.

prep + cook time 25 minutes (+ cooling) **serves** 4

nutritional count per serving

▶ 9.5g total fat   ▶ 42g carbohydrate
▶ 3.1g saturated fat   ▶ 27.5g protein
▶ 1588kJ (379 cal)   ▶ 6.9g fibre

tip This sandwich is at its best eaten warm, but if you don't have the right facilities to cook the chicken and bacon at lunch time, then cook them in the morning and assemble the sandwich at work.

chicken and bacon club

1 chicken breast fillet (200g)

cooking-oil spray

4 shortcut bacon rashers (60g)

⅔ cup (130g) low-fat cottage cheese

8 slices rye bread (360g), toasted

40g (1½ ounces) baby rocket leaves (arugula)

1 large tomato (220g), sliced thinly

1 Lightly spray chicken with oil. Heat a medium frying pan over medium heat; cook chicken about 5 minutes each side or until cooked through. Remove from heat; cover, rest 5 minutes, then slice thinly.

2 Cook bacon in the same pan until crisp.

3 Divide half the cheese between four toast slices; top with rocket, tomato, chicken, bacon, remaining cheese and toast.

prep + cook time 20 minutes **serves** 4

ham, tomato and avocado open sandwich

4 medium roma (egg) tomatoes (300g), halved

2 tablespoons brown sugar

8 slices ciabatta bread (280g), toasted

1 small avocado (200g), sliced thinly

200g (6½ ounces) shaved ham

1 Preheat oven to 200°C/400°F.

2 Place tomato, cut-side up, on an oven tray, sprinkle with sugar; roast, uncovered, for 15 minutes.

3 Top toast slices with avocado, ham and tomato; season.

prep + cook time 20 minutes **serves** 4

tip Tomatoes can be roasted a day ahead; store, covered, in the fridge. If taking to work, assemble just before serving.

roast beef and horseradish cream wraps

1 cup (240g) char-grilled capsicum (bell pepper)

1 tablespoon horseradish cream

4 rye mountain bread wraps (120g)

300g (9½ ounces) sliced rare roast beef

100g (3 ounces) baby rocket leaves (arugula)

1 Drain capsicum well; pat dry with kitchen paper.

2 Spread horseradish over each wrap.

3 Divide beef, capsicum and rocket between wraps. Roll to enclose filling.

prep time 5 minutes **serves** 4

tips Roast beef can be swapped with corned silverside or pastrami. The wrap can be made on the morning of serving, make sure the capsicum doesn't come in contact with the bread as it may turn soggy.

nutritional count per serving

▸ 9.8g total fat ▸ 51.1g carbohydrate
▸ 2.6g saturated fat ▸ 25g protein
▸ 1731kJ (415 cal) ▸ 9.7g fibre

roast beef and coleslaw on rye

2 cups (160g) finely shredded cabbage

1 large carrot (180g), grated coarsely

4 green onions (scallions), chopped finely

½ cup (150g) low-fat mayonnaise

2 tablespoons lemon juice

8 slices rare roast beef (240g)

8 slices rye bread (360g)

1 Combine cabbage, carrot, onion, mayonnaise and juice in a medium bowl.
2 Divide beef between four slices of bread; top with coleslaw, then remaining bread.

prep time 20 minutes **serves** 4

tips You can buy the roast beef, already cooked and sliced, from any deli. Make the coleslaw the night before, and make the sandwich at lunch time the next day.

Use whatever cabbage you like; we used red cabbage, but try the chinese variety (wombok), it's easy to shred finely.

nutritional count per serving

▶ 8.1g total fat ▶ 57.1g carbohydrate
▶ 2.1g saturated fat ▶ 29.7g protein
▶ 1828kJ (437 cal) ▶ 6.6g fibre

salmon pasta salad

2 cups (300g) spiral pasta

340g (11 ounces) asparagus, trimmed, chopped coarsely

¼ cup (60g) low-fat ricotta

2 teaspoons finely grated lemon rind

½ cup (125ml) lemon juice

2 cloves garlic, crushed

1 large red capsicum (bell pepper) (350g), sliced thinly

⅔ cup coarsely chopped fresh flat-leaf parsley

4 green onions (scallions), sliced thinly

415g (13-ounce) can pink salmon in springwater, drained, flaked

1 Cook pasta in a medium saucepan of boiling water until just tender. Add asparagus; cook 1 minute. Drain.
2 Meanwhile, combine ricotta, rind, juice and garlic in a large bowl; add pasta, asparagus and remaining ingredients. Toss to combine, season to taste.

prep + cook time 20 minutes **serves** 4

tips Choose any pasta you like. This salad can be eaten hot or cold. If you want to take it to work for lunch, make it the night before; store, covered, in the fridge.

healthy sides

broccolini with honey

Steam 700g (1½ pounds) broccolini in a large baking-paper-lined steamer, over a large saucepan of simmering water, for about 5 minutes or until tender. Meanwhile, combine 1 tablespoon each of light soy sauce and water, and 2 teaspoons honey in a small jug. Serve broccolini drizzled with sauce and sprinkled with 2 teaspoons toasted sesame seeds.

prep + cook time 10 minutes **serves** 4
nutritional count per serving 1.3g total fat (0g saturated fat); 326kJ (78 cal); 4.1g carbohydrate; 8.8g protein; 7.3g fibre

squash and zucchini with leek dressing

To make leek dressing, heat 2 teaspoons olive oil in a small frying pan over medium-high heat; cook 1 thinly sliced small leek, stirring, about 10 minutes or until tender. Remove from heat; stir in 2 tablespoons lemon juice, 1 tablespoon each of vegetable stock and rice vinegar, and 2 teaspoons lemon thyme leaves. Meanwhile, steam 8 quartered medium yellow patty-pan squash and 12 baby zucchini in a medium baking-paper-lined steamer, over a medium saucepan of simmering water, for about 5 minutes or until tender. Drizzle vegetables with dressing.

prep + cook time 15 minutes **serves** 4
nutritional count per serving 2.7g total fat (0.3g saturated fat); 247kJ (59 cal); 4.3g carbohydrate; 2.9g protein; 3.1g fibre

tip If baby zucchini are unavailable, cut small zucchini into quarters.

dill and lemon potatoes

Steam 600g (1¼ pounds) halved baby new potatoes in a medium baking-paper-lined steamer, over a medium saucepan of simmering water, for about 25 minutes or until tender. Meanwhile, combine 2 tablespoons lemon juice, 1 tablespoon coarsely chopped fresh dill, 2 teaspoons each of dijon mustard and olive oil, and ½ teaspoon white (granulated) sugar in a screw-top jar; shake well. Combine potatoes and dressing in a large bowl. Serve topped with extra dill, if you like.

prep + cook time 35 minutes **serves** 4
nutritional count per serving 2.5g total fat (0.3g saturated fat); 527kJ (126 cal); 20.5g carbohydrate; 3.7g protein; 3.1g fibre

steamed asian vegetables

Steam 300g (9½ ounces) gai lan, 1 thickly sliced medium capsicum and 1 thickly sliced large carrot in a large baking-paper-lined steamer, over a large saucepan of simmering water, for 3 minutes. Add 150g (4½ ounces) trimmed snow peas; cook about 2 minutes or until vegetables are tender. Meanwhile, combine 2 tablespoons light soy sauce, 1cm (½-inch) piece of grated ginger, 1 finely chopped fresh small red thai (serrano) chilli and ½ teaspoon sesame oil in a screw-top jar; shake well. Drizzle vegetables with dressing.

prep + cook time 15 minutes **serves** 4
nutritional count per serving 0.9g total fat (0.1g saturated fat); 226kJ (54 cal); 6.2g carbohydrate; 3.4g protein; 3.5g fibre

lunch weekends

spiced lamb cutlets with tomato and herb salad

2 teaspoons ground cumin

1 tablespoon each ground coriander and paprika

8 french-trimmed lamb cutlets (400g)

800g (1½ pounds) mixed baby tomatoes, halved

1 small red onion (100g), sliced thinly

⅓ cup each firmly packed fresh flat-leaf parsley and small basil leaves

2 tablespoons lemon juice

120g (2 ounces) mesclun

2 tablespoons balsamic glaze

4 large pitta breads (320g), toasted, torn into pieces

lemon wedges, for serving

1 Combine spices in a small bowl; sprinkle spice mixture over both sides of cutlets.

2 Heat a large non-stick frying pan over medium heat; cook cutlets about 3 minutes each side or until cooked as desired.

3 Meanwhile, combine tomato, onion, herbs and juice in a small bowl; season to taste. Place mesclun in another small bowl; drizzle over balsamic glaze.

4 Serve lamb with salads, bread and lemon wedges.

prep + cook time 20 minutes **serves** 4

tip These cutlets are delicious served cold with the salad but, if you prefer, you can reheat them, covered, in a microwave oven on HIGH (100%), for about 1 minute.

pappardelle with fresh tomato sauce

1 large red onion (300g), chopped finely

2 cloves garlic, crushed

½ cup coarsely chopped fresh basil

2 tablespoons red wine vinegar

10 medium tomatoes (1.5kg), chopped finely

300g (9½ ounces) pappardelle pasta

120g (4 ounces) baby rocket leaves (arugula)

½ cup (120g) low-fat ricotta, crumbled

1 Combine onion, garlic, basil, vinegar and tomato in a medium bowl; stand 10 minutes.

2 Meanwhile, cook pasta in a large saucepan of boiling water until just tender; drain. Return pasta to pan; add tomato mixture and rocket, mix gently.

3 Top pasta with cheese; serve immediately.

prep + cook time 20 minutes **serves** 4

serving suggestion Serve with garlic bread; 2 slices will add 706kJ (168 cal) to each serve.

tip This recipe is a delicious change to cooked pasta sauces – because this sauce is uncooked, buy the freshest ingredients you can for a big flavour hit.

nutritional count per serving

▶ 14.8g total fat   ▶ 10.4g carbohydrate
▶ 4.6g saturated fat   ▶ 37.1g protein
▶ 1388kJ (331 cal)   ▶ 3.4g fibre

tips Some butchers sell a pork and veal mixture, however, if it is not available as a mixture, buy half the amount as pork mince and half the amount as veal mince. Tap the stem end of a cored iceberg lettuce soundly against the edge of the kitchen sink, then hold the lettuce under cold running water; the leaves will fall off, one by one, intact.

sang choy bow

1 teaspoon sesame oil

1 medium brown onion (150g), chopped finely

1 clove garlic, crushed

600g (1¼ ounces) minced (ground) pork and veal mixture

¼ cup (60ml) light soy sauce

¼ cup (60ml) oyster sauce

1 medium red capsicum (bell pepper) (200g), chopped finely

3 cups (240g) bean sprouts

4 green onions (scallions), chopped coarsely

8 large iceberg lettuce leaves

1 tablespoon toasted sesame seeds

1 Heat oil in a wok; stir-fry brown onion and garlic, over medium heat, until onion softens. Add mince; stir-fry until cooked through. Add sauces and capsicum; reduce heat, simmer, uncovered, stirring occasionally, for 3 minutes.
2 Just before serving, stir sprouts and green onion into the mixture. Divide sang choy bow into lettuce leaves; sprinkle with sesame seeds to serve.

prep + cook time 25 minutes **serves** 4

serving suggestion Serve sprinkled with thinly sliced chilli and coriander leaves (cilantro).

Sang choy bow is China's answer to the hamburger – this delicious hand-held lunch uses the common iceberg lettuce because its cupped leaf is a perfect vessel for the filling.

chilli prawn noodle salad

1kg (2 pounds) unshelled cooked medium prawns (shrimp)

⅓ cup (80ml) lime juice

2 tablespoons sweet chilli sauce

1 fresh long red chilli, sliced thinly

1 fresh long green chilli, sliced thinly

1 teaspoon white (granulated) sugar

200g (6½ ounces) bean thread noodles

1 cup firmly packed fresh mint leaves

100g (3 ounces) snow pea sprouts

1 Shell and devein prawns, leaving tails intact. Combine prawns in a large bowl with juice, sauce, chillies and sugar.
2 Place noodles in a large heatproof bowl, cover with boiling water; stand until tender, drain.
3 Add noodles to prawn mixture with mint and sprouts; toss gently to combine.

prep time 30 minutes   **serves** 4

tip We served the salad on butter lettuce leaves, however, this is optional.

Prawns have a rich flavour and moist flesh. They are low in saturated fat and high in protein

tips Under-ripe tomatoes should be left at room temperature to ripen and develop colour and flavour. All tomatoes should be taken out of the fridge at least half an hour before use. Smoked almonds are available from most major supermarkets.

roasted pumpkin and tomato soup

1.2kg (2½ pounds) pumpkin, cut into 2cm (¾-inch) pieces

cooking-oil spray

1 medium red onion (170g), chopped finely

2 medium ripe tomatoes (300g), chopped finely

2 cloves garlic, crushed

¼ cup (70g) tomato paste

⅔ cup (130g) brown rice

2 cups (500ml) water

1.5 litres (6 cups) chicken or vegetable stock

2 tablespoons coarsely chopped smoked almonds

1 Preheat oven to 200°C/400°F.

2 Place pumpkin in a medium baking dish; spray with oil. Roast about 20 minutes or until pumpkin is browned lightly.

3 Meanwhile, heat a lightly oiled medium saucepan over medium heat; cook onion, tomato and garlic, stirring, until onion is soft. Stir in paste, rice, the water and stock; bring to the boil. Reduce heat; simmer soup, uncovered, for about 30 minutes or until rice is tender.

4 Divide pumpkin among serving bowls; top with soup, sprinkle with almonds to serve. Top with fresh thyme, if you like.

prep + cook time 50 minutes **serves** 4

serving suggestion Add 4 slices shortcut bacon to the recipe for added flavour; this will add 363kJ (87 cal) to each serve.

nutritional count per serving

▶ 7.4g total fat   ▶ 29.9g carbohydrate
▶ 1.7g saturated fat   ▶ 58.8g protein
▶ 1463kJ (350 cal)   ▶ 9g fibre

tip Burghul is a par-boiled whole wheat with a mild, nutty taste. It is high in fibre, and its chewy texture helps keep hunger at bay.

chicken tabbouleh

1 cup (160g) burghul

12 chicken tenderloins (900g)

4 medium tomatoes (600g), chopped finely

2 lebanese cucumbers (260g), seeded, chopped finely

6 green onions (scallions), sliced thinly

1 cup finely chopped fresh flat-leaf parsley

⅓ cup (80ml) lemon juice

1 clove garlic, crushed

⅔ cup (190g) skim-milk yoghurt

lemon wedges, to serve

1 Dry-fry burghul in a large non-stick frying pan over medium heat, stirring, about 2 minutes or until browned lightly. Transfer to a medium heatproof bowl. Cover burghul with boiling water; stand about 10 minutes or until burghul is tender. Drain burghul; squeeze out excess liquid, return burghul to bowl.
2 Cook chicken in the same heated pan, over medium heat, for 3 minutes each side or until cooked through.
3 To make tabbouleh; stir tomato, cucumber, onion, parsley, juice and garlic into burghul; season to taste. Serve tabbouleh with chicken, yoghurt and lemon wedges.

prep + cook time 20 minutes **serves** 4

Tabbouleh is full of fresh flavours and is high in fibre – it can be eaten on its own, but the chicken adds protein to the dish.

vegetable and red lentil soup

2 tablespoons curry paste

800g (1½ pounds) canned diced tomatoes

3 cups (750ml) chicken stock

1 medium carrot (120g), chopped finely

2 stalks celery (300g), trimmed, chopped finely

2 small potatoes (240g), chopped finely

2 small zucchini (180g), chopped finely

⅔ cup (130g) dried red lentils

½ cup (60g) frozen peas

⅓ cup (95g) low-fat plain yoghurt

⅓ cup coarsely chopped fresh coriander leaves (cilantro)

1 Cook curry paste in a heated large saucepan, stirring, about 1 minute or until fragrant. Stir in tomatoes, stock, carrot, celery, potato and zucchini; bring to the boil. Reduce heat; simmer, covered, for 5 minutes.

2 Add lentils to soup mixture; return to the boil. Reduce heat; simmer, uncovered, about 10 minutes or until lentils are just tender. Add peas; return to the boil. Reduce heat; simmer, uncovered, until peas are just tender.

3 Remove soup from heat; top with yoghurt and coriander to serve.

prep + cook time 30 minutes **serves** 4

serving suggestion Serve soup with a small piece of naan bread; this will add 1145kJ (273 cal) to each serve.

tips While a hot curry paste, or some finely chopped chilli, will boost the flavour, you can use any curry paste you like. This soup can be made up to 2 days ahead. The lentils will absorb the liquid, so you may need to add some extra water or stock while reheating.

nutritional count per serving

▶ 13.7g total fat   ▶ 29.6g carbohydrate
▶ 4.1g saturated fat   ▶ 13.6g protein
▶ 1285kJ (307 cal)   ▶ 5.7g fibre

spinach and cheese quesadillas

⅓ cup (65g) low-fat cottage cheese

50g (1½ ounces) baby spinach leaves

1 small avocado (200g), chopped finely

½ cup (100g) canned kidney beans, rinsed, drained

125g (4 ounces) canned corn kernels, rinsed, drained

1 medium tomato (150g), seeded, chopped finely

1 small red onion (100g), chopped finely

1 medium zucchini (120g), grated coarsely

8 x 15cm (6-inch) flour tortillas

½ cup (50g) coarsely grated reduced-fat mozzarella

2 tablespoons loosely packed fresh coriander leaves (cilantro)

1 Blend or process cottage cheese and spinach until smooth.
2 Combine avocado, beans, corn, tomato, onion and zucchini in a medium bowl.
3 Preheat grill (broiler).
4 Place four tortillas on oven trays; spread spinach mixture over tortillas, leaving a 2cm (¾-inch) border around the edge. Spread avocado mixture over spinach mixture; top each with the remaining tortillas.
5 Sprinkle mozzarella over quesadilla stacks. Grill quesadillas until browned lightly. Serve sprinkled with coriander.

prep + cook time 40 minutes   **serves** 4

serving suggestion Serve with corn salsa, see recipe page 85.

tip Quesadillas can be cooked in a heated sandwich press, just make sure you gently wrap the quesadilla in baking paper before pressing, to stop the filling from burning the press.

tips Use disposable gloves when handling beetroot to stop it staining your hands. If taking to work, pack patties, vegies, bun and relish separately; reheat the patties in a microwave oven on HIGH (100%) for about 1 minute before assembling.

zucchini burger

4 medium zucchini (480g), grated coarsely

⅔ cup (70g) packaged breadcrumbs

2 tablespoons finely grated parmesan

2 green onions (scallions), sliced thinly

2 egg whites, beaten lightly

2 tablespoons finely chopped fresh flat-leaf parsley

cooking-oil spray

1 large brown onion (200g), sliced thinly

8 green oak leaf lettuce leaves

2 small fresh beetroot (beets) (200g), peeled, grated coarsely

⅓ cup (110g) tomato relish

4 hamburger buns (360g), split, toasted

1 Place zucchini in a strainer; squeeze excess water from zucchini. Combine zucchini, breadcrumbs, parmesan, onion, egg white and parsley in a medium bowl; season. Shape mixture into four patties.

2 Spray a medium frying pan with oil; cook onion, stirring, for about 10 minutes or until browned lightly. Remove from pan.

3 Cook patties in same pan until browned both sides and heated through.

4 Sandwich lettuce, patties, onion, beetroot and relish between bun halves.

prep + cook time 40 minutes **serves** 4

healthy sides

roasted tomatoes with garlic and herbs

Preheat oven to 200°C/400°F. Place 6 halved large roma (egg) tomatoes, cut-side up, in a single layer, in a large baking dish. Combine 1 teaspoon sea salt, 1 teaspoon cracked black pepper, 6 sprigs fresh thyme, 1 clove thinly sliced garlic and 3 teaspoons olive oil; drizzle over tomato. Roast, uncovered, for 1 hour or until the tomato softens and browns lightly. Drizzle tomato with combined 1½ teaspoons finely chopped fresh oregano, ½ teaspoon finely chopped fresh thyme and 1½ tablespoons olive oil.

prep + cook time 1¼ hours **serves** 4
nutritional count per serving 9.3g total fat (1.3g saturated fat); 426kJ (102 cal); 2.7g carbohydrate; 1.4g protein; 1.8g fibre

tip Roast the tomatoes in a baking dish with deep sides; this shields them from the heat so they won't burn.

roasted baby carrots with garlic

Preheat oven to 220°C/425°F. Trim tops of 2 bunches of baby carrots, leaving 2cm (¾-inch) of the stems intact. Wash carrots well. Place carrots in a medium baking dish; combine 1 tablespoon olive oil, 1 clove crushed garlic and 2 teaspoons honey; pour over carrots, toss well. Roast, uncovered, for 15 minutes. Add 2 teaspoons fresh thyme leaves; roast for a further 3 minutes or until tender.

prep + cook time 35 minutes **serves** 4
nutritional count per serving 4.7g total fat (0.7g saturated fat); 355kJ (85 cal); 8.1g carbohydrate; 0.9g protein; 4.1g fibre

mixed garlic mushrooms

Preheat oven to 200°C/400°F. Place 200g (6½ ounces) flat mushrooms in a large baking dish, drizzle with 1 tablespoon olive oil; roast, uncovered, 10 minutes. Add 200g (6½ ounces) each swiss brown and button mushrooms, 2 teaspoons olive oil and 1 thinly sliced garlic clove to dish; roast, uncovered, a further 15 minutes or until mushrooms are tender and browned lightly. Stir in ¼ cup loosely packed fresh flat-leaf parsley leaves.

prep + cook time 30 minutes **serves** 4
nutritional count per serving 7.3g total fat
(1.1g saturated fat); 441kJ (105 cal); 2.4g carbohydrate;
5.6g protein; 4.3g fibre

rosemary potatoes

Preheat oven to 180°C/350°F. Make 1cm (½-inch) cuts in 1kg (2 pounds) potatoes, slicing about three-quarters of the way through. Combine potatoes with 2 teaspoons olive oil in a large baking dish; sprinkle with salt and freshly ground black pepper. Roast, uncovered, about 1 hour. Increase oven temperature to 220°C/425°F. Roast potatoes a further 15 minutes or until browned and tender. Sprinkle with 2 teaspoons fresh rosemary leaves.

prep + cook time 1¾ hours **serves** 4
nutritional count per serving 2.5g total fat
(0.3g saturated fat); 759kJ (181 cal); 30.8g carbohydrate;
5.8g protein; 4.2g fibre

dinner

You've been good all day, so don't blow it now. These dinners may be filling, but there will still be room for dessert.

dinner
weekdays

linguine marinara

300g (9½ ounces) linguine pasta

800g (1½ pounds) marinara mix

1 medium brown onion (150g), chopped finely

3 cloves garlic, crushed

2 fresh small red thai (serrano) chillies, chopped finely

800g (1½ pounds) canned diced tomatoes

⅔ cup coarsely chopped fresh flat-leaf parsley

1 Cook pasta in a large saucepan of boiling water until just tender; drain.

2 Meanwhile, cook marinara mix in a heated large frying pan, over high heat, stirring, for 2 minutes; remove from pan, drain.

3 Add onion, garlic and chilli to same heated pan; cook, stirring, for 5 minutes or until onion softens. Add tomatoes; cook, stirring, for 5 minutes. Return seafood to pan; cook, stirring occasionally, for 2 minutes or until heated through. Stir in parsley.

4 Serve pasta with marinara sauce.

prep + cook time 20 minutes **serves** 4

nutritional count per serving

▶ 7.2g total fat   ▶ 61.9g carbohydrate
▶ 1.8g saturated fat ▶ 60.1g protein
▶ 2387kJ (571 cal)   ▶ 6.4g fibre

tips This is a really simple recipe. There's only one thing to be careful of – don't overcook the seafood, because, if you do, it will be tough and leathery. Use any pasta shape you like – and don't overcook it either; cooked pasta with a little bit of bite is better for your digestive system.

Swap the lamb mince for beef or chicken mince.

nutritional count per serving

▸ 8.6g total fat
▸ 2.4g saturated fat
▸ 1688kJ (403 cal)
▸ 41g carbohydrate
▸ 35.7g protein
▸ 6.4g fibre

tips You could use oregano instead of rosemary. Patties can be made 3 days ahead; store, covered, in the fridge, or freeze for up to 3 months.

mediterranean lamb burgers

6 lamb fillets (400g), chopped coarsely

2 egg whites

1 cup (70g) stale wholemeal breadcrumbs

1 tablespoon fresh rosemary sprigs

1 tablespoon firmly packed fresh mint leaves

2 teaspoons finely grated lemon rind

1 clove garlic, quartered

1 tablespoon tomato paste

cooking-oil spray

100g (9½ ounces) mixed salad leaves

1 medium tomato (150g), sliced thinly

1 medium red onion (170g), sliced thinly

4 wholemeal bread rolls (280g) split in half

yoghurt sauce

⅔ cup (190g) low-fat plain yoghurt

1 clove garlic, crushed

2 tablespoons finely chopped fresh mint leaves

1 lebanese cucumber (130g), seeded, chopped finely

1 Process lamb, egg white, breadcrumbs, herbs, rind, garlic and paste until smooth. Using wet hands, shape mixture into four equal-sized patties.

2 Lightly spray a heated large non-stick frying pan with oil; cook patties, over medium heat, for 4 minutes each side or until browned and cooked through.

3 Make yoghurt sauce.

4 Sandwich salad leaves, tomato, patties, onion and yoghurt sauce between rolls.

yoghurt sauce Combine ingredients in a small bowl.

prep + cook time 25 minutes **serves** 4

serving suggestion Serve with some homemade oven-baked potato and kumara wedges.

tip Any asian greens can be used in this recipe. Try it with buk choy or gai lan (also known as chinese broccoli); you need one bunch of asian greens. Add some baby spinach leaves and cucumber ribbons to the salad, if you like.

warm pork and choy sum salad

800g (1½ pounds) pork tenderloin

⅓ cup (80ml) lime juice

2cm (¾-inch) piece fresh ginger (10g), grated

2 medium carrots (240g)

cooking-oil spray

500g (1 pound) choy sum, chopped coarsely

2 tablespoons water

½ cup firmly packed fresh basil leaves

1 cup firmly packed fresh coriander leaves (cilantro)

4 green onions (scallions), sliced thinly

sweet chilli dressing

1 tablespoon fish sauce

1 tablespoon sweet chilli sauce

1 tablespoon lime juice

1 fresh small red thai (serrano) chilli, chopped finely

1 Place pork in a large bowl with juice and ginger; toss to coat pork in mixture.

2 Make sweet chilli dressing.

3 Using a vegetable peeler, slice carrot into thin ribbons.

4 Lightly spray a medium frying pan with oil; cook pork over medium heat about 8 minutes or until browned all over and cooked as desired. Remove from pan; cover to keep warm.

5 Add choy sum to same heated pan with the water; cook, stirring, until choy sum is just wilted.

6 Meanwhile, thickly slice pork. Place choy sum, carrot, herbs and onion in a large bowl with dressing; toss gently. Serve pork with salad.

sweet chilli dressing Combine ingredients in a screw-top jar; shake well.

prep + cook time 35 minutes **serves** 4

serving suggestion Toss cooked rice stick noodles through the salad.

lamb and lentil curry

1 cup (200g) yellow split peas

cooking-oil spray

600g (1¼ pounds) lamb fillets, cut into 4cm (1½-inch) pieces

1 large brown onion (200g), sliced thinly

2cm (¾-inch) piece fresh ginger (10g), chopped finely

1 clove garlic, crushed

1 tablespoon ground coriander

1 teaspoon hot paprika

¼ teaspoon cayenne pepper

2 medium tomatoes (300g), chopped coarsely

⅓ cup (160ml) light coconut cream

1½ cups (375ml) chicken stock

150g (4½ ounces) baby spinach leaves

12 mini pappadums (40g)

½ cup coarsely chopped fresh coriander (cilantro)

⅓ cup (95g) low-fat plain yoghurt

1 Place split peas in a medium saucepan, cover with water; bring to the boil. Reduce heat, simmer, uncovered, for about 30 minutes or until tender; drain.

2 Meanwhile, lightly spray a large frying pan with oil; cook lamb, stirring, over medium heat, about 4 minutes or until cooked as desired. Remove from pan.

3 Cook onion in same heated pan, stirring, about 5 minutes or until softened. Add ginger, garlic, ground coriander, paprika and cayenne; cook, stirring, until fragrant.

4 Add tomato, coconut cream and stock to the pan; bring to the boil. Reduce heat; simmer, covered, about 5 minutes or until sauce thickens slightly.

5 Return lamb to pan with split peas and spinach; cook, stirring, until heated through.

6 Cook pappadums according to packet directions; serve with curry, fresh coriander and yoghurt.

prep + cook time 35 minutes **serves** 4

tips The curry can be made a day ahead; store, covered, in the fridge. You may need to add a little water when reheating the curry, as the split peas will soak up the liquid. Substitute lamb with beef or chicken, if you prefer.

tips You could add snow peas or beans to the stir-fry. Partially freeze the chicken; this makes it easier to slice thinly.

stir-fry thai chicken

200g (6½ ounces) wide dried rice stick noodles

1 teaspoon olive oil

300g (9½ ounces) chicken breast fillet, sliced thinly

200g (6½ ounces) green beans, halved

2 cloves garlic, crushed

2cm (¾-inch) piece fresh ginger (10g), grated

2 tablespoons sweet chilli sauce

2 tablespoons water

500g (1 pound) baby buk choy, halved lengthways

1 tablespoon fish sauce

2 tablespoons lime juice

6 green onions (scallions), sliced thinly

1 cup bean sprouts (80g)

1 cup firmly packed fresh coriander leaves (cilantro)

1 cup firmly packed fresh mint leaves

1 fresh small red thai (serrano) chilli, sliced thinly

1 Place noodles in a large heatproof bowl, cover with boiling water; stand until just tender, drain.
2 Meanwhile, heat oil in a wok over medium heat; stir-fry chicken until just cooked. Add beans, garlic, ginger, sweet chilli sauce and the water to wok; stir-fry until beans are almost tender.
3 Add buk choy, fish sauce, juice, onion, sprouts and half the herbs to wok; stir-fry until hot.
4 Serve chicken mixture on noodles; sprinkle with chilli and remaining herbs. Accompany with lime wedges, if you like.

prep + cook time 35 minutes   **serves** 4

tips Wontons can be made a day ahead, cover with damp kitchen paper and plastic wrap; store in the fridge. The choy sum can be substituted with buk choy. To lessen the heat of this recipe, remove the seeds from the chilli.

chive wontons with choy sum in asian broth

100g (3 ounces) firm silken tofu

200g (6½ ounces) choy sum, trimmed

1 tablespoon finely chopped fresh chives

230g (7 ounces) canned water chestnuts, rinsed, drained, chopped finely

1 fresh long red chilli, chopped finely

24 square wonton wrappers

3 cups (750ml) vegetable stock

3 cups (750ml) water

5cm (2-inch) stick fresh lemon grass (10g), chopped coarsely

2cm (¾-inch) piece fresh ginger (10g), chopped coarsely

1 clove garlic, quartered

1 kaffir lime leaf

1½ tablespoons light soy sauce

1 Dry tofu with kitchen paper then chop coarsely. Stand tofu on several layers of kitchen paper, cover with more paper; stand for 20 minutes, then chop finely.

2 Chop a quarter of the choy sum finely. Combine in a medium bowl with tofu, chives, water chestnut and half the chilli.

3 Centre a level tablespoon of tofu mixture on a wonton wrapper. Brush edges with water; gather edges above filling, pinching together to seal. Repeat process with remaining wrappers and filling to make a total of 24 wontons.

4 Combine stock, the water, lemon grass, ginger, garlic, lime leaf, sauce and remaining chilli in a large saucepan; bring to the boil. Reduce heat; simmer, uncovered, for 5 minutes. Strain into a large bowl; discard solids.

5 Return broth to pan; bring to the boil; cook wontons, in two batches, about 4 minutes or until cooked through. Transfer wontons to individual serving bowls.

6 Cook remaining choy sum in broth until just tender. Divide choy sum among bowls; ladle broth over choy sum and wontons.

prep + cook time 55 minutes (+ standing) **serves** 4

nutritional count per serving

- ▶ 4.7g total fat
- ▶ 1.7g saturated fat
- ▶ 1605kJ (384 cal)
- ▶ 16.4g carbohydrate
- ▶ 36.1g protein
- ▶ 2.5g fibre

beef with red wine and kumara mash

4 cloves garlic, unpeeled

3 cups (750ml) dry red wine

2 cups (500ml) water

8 sprigs fresh thyme

600g (1¼ pound) piece middle-cut beef eye fillet, trimmed, tied at 3cm (1¼-inch) intervals

kumara mash

1 large kumara (orange sweet potato) (500g), unpeeled

¼ cup (60ml) fresh orange juice, strained

1 teaspoon fresh thyme leaves

1 Bruise unpeeled garlic by hitting it with the flat blade of a large heavy knife.

2 Combine garlic, wine, the water and thyme in a large deep saucepan; bring to the boil, boil for 5 minutes. Add beef; simmer, uncovered, about 20 minutes (for medium-rare) or until cooked as desired, turning beef once. Remove beef, wrap in foil; rest for 10 minutes before slicing thinly.

3 Meanwhile, make kumara mash.

4 Serve beef with kumara mash; accompany with wholegrain (seeded) mustard, if you like.

kumara mash Boil, steam or microwave kumara until tender; cool. Peel kumara, place in a large saucepan; roughly mash with a fork. Add juice and thyme; stir over medium heat until hot. Season to taste.

prep + cook time 30 minutes **serves** 4

serving suggestion Serve with green beans or wilted silver beet.

nutritional count per serving

▶ 5.3g total fat
▶ 1.4g saturated fat
▶ 1660kJ (397 cal)

▶ 42.4g carbohydrate
▶ 41g protein
▶ 6.1g fibre

tips Use any firm fish that's in season. Sumac is a Middle-Eastern spice with a tart flavour; it's available from most supermarkets. Substitute the sumac in this recipe with 2½ teaspoons lemon pepper, ¾ teaspoon chinese five-spice powder and ¾ teaspoon all spice.

sumac fish with couscous salad

cooking-oil spray

1 medium red onion (170g), chopped finely

2 cloves garlic, crushed

2 large zucchini (300g), sliced diagonally

250g (8 ounces) cherry or grape tomatoes

½ cup coarsely chopped fresh mint

1 cup (250ml) vegetable stock

1 cup (200g) couscous

640g (¼ pounds) firm white fish fillets

1 tablespoon sumac

lemon wedges, for serving

1 Spray a medium frying pan with oil; cook onion and garlic, stirring, over medium heat, for 1 minute. Add zucchini and tomatoes; cook, stirring occasionally, about 10 minutes or until vegetables soften. Remove from heat; stir in mint.
2 Bring stock to the boil in a small saucepan; remove from heat, stir in couscous. Stand, covered, for 5 minutes or until liquid is absorbed, fluffing with a fork occasionally. Stir couscous into zucchini mixture.
3 Meanwhile, preheat grill (broiler). Sprinkle fish with sumac; Grill for about 3 minutes each side or until cooked through.
4 Serve couscous topped with fish; accompany with wedges.

prep + cook time 30 minutes **serves** 4

nutritional count per serving

▶ 7.4g total fat   ▶ 48.4g carbohydrate
▶ 2.4g saturated fat   ▶ 36.1g protein
▶ 1793kJ (428 cal)   ▶ 8.7g fibre

tips Swap beef with chicken, pork or lamb. Stir-fries are best made just before serving. Partially freeze the steak before cutting; this makes it easier to slice thinly.

sesame beef stir-fry

1 cup (200g) couscous

1 cup (250ml) boiling water

1 tablespoon sesame seeds

400g (12½ ounces) beef rump steak, sliced thinly

1 medium red onion (170g), cut into wedges

2 cloves garlic, crushed

2 baby buk choy (300g), quartered

1 fresh long red chilli, sliced thinly

⅓ cup (80ml) beef stock

⅓ cup (80ml) oyster sauce

⅓ cup (80ml) light soy sauce

300g (9½ ounces) snow peas, sliced thinly

1 Combine couscous with the boiling water in a medium heatproof bowl, cover; stand for 5 minutes or until liquid is absorbed, fluffing with a fork occasionally.
2 Meanwhile, toast sesame seeds in a heated wok about 30 seconds; transfer to a small bowl.
3 Stir-fry beef in heated wok, over high heat, in batches, until browned; transfer to a small bowl.
4 Stir-fry onion in same heated wok for 1 minute. Add garlic, buk choy and chilli; stir-fry 1 minute. Add stock, sauces and beef; stir-fry until hot. Remove from heat; stir in peas.
5 Top couscous with stir-fry; serve sprinkled with sesame seeds.

prep + cook time 20 minutes **serves** 4

Add a herb like coriander or
basil for a bit more flavour.

For an extra hit of vegetables,
add some mixed salad leaves,
baby rocket or baby spinach
to the salad.

tip Chickpea purée can be made a day ahead; store, covered, in the fridge. Reheat in a microwave oven on MEDIUM (50%) in 30 second bursts until heated through.

pork cutlets with chickpea purée

400g (12½ ounces) canned chickpeas, rinsed, drained

¼ cup (60ml) lemon juice

2 cloves garlic, crushed

1 teaspoon ground fennel

½ cup (125ml) warm water

4 pork cutlets (940g), trimmed

cooking-oil spray

10 red radishes (600g), cut into matchsticks

2 lebanese cucumbers (260g), chopped coarsely

½ cup coarsely chopped fresh flat-leaf parsley

1 Process chickpeas, juice, garlic and fennel until combined. Add the water; process until smooth.
2 Spray pork with oil; cook pork on a heated grill plate (or grill or barbecue) for about 5 minutes each side or until cooked as desired. Cover, rest for 5 minutes.
3 Meanwhile, combine remaining ingredients in a medium bowl.
4 Serve pork with salad and chickpea purée.

prep + cook time 20 minutes **serves** 4

serving suggestion Make some croûtons by cutting 2 slices of sourdough into cubes and grilling, or dry-frying, in a frying pan, until golden. Toss them through the salad; this will add 154kJ (37 cal) per serve.

tips Use only the rind from the preserved lemon; rinse the rind well under cold water then drain, dry and finely chop. Bulk up the tomato salad by adding some baby spinach leaves.

zucchini fritters with tomato mint salad

6 medium zucchini (720g)

1 medium brown onion (150g), chopped finely

1¼ cups (85g) stale breadcrumbs

3 egg whites

1 tablespoon finely chopped fresh oregano

1 teaspoon sumac

cooking-oil spray

⅓ cup (95g) low-fat natural yoghurt

2 teaspoons finely chopped preserved lemon rind

tomato mint salad

200g (6½ ounces) red grape tomatoes, quartered

200g (6½ ounces) yellow grape tomatoes, quartered

⅓ cup firmly packed fresh mint leaves

1 Coarsely grate zucchini; squeeze and discard excess liquid from zucchini.

2 Combine zucchini, onion, breadcrumbs, egg whites, oregano and sumac in a medium bowl.

3 Lightly spray a heated large frying pan (or barbecue flat plate) with oil. Drop heaped tablespoons of zucchini mixture into pan; using a metal spatula, flatten fritters slightly. Cook, over medium heat, about 2 minutes each side or until fritters are cooked through. Remove from pan; cover to keep warm. Repeat with remaining mixture to make a total of 16 fritters.

4 Meanwhile, make tomato mint salad. Serve fritters with salad and combined yoghurt and preserved lemon.

tomato mint salad Combine ingredients in a medium bowl.

prep + cook time 35 minutes **serves** 4

Ruby red is just a pink version of grapefruit. Use orange or blood orange segments, if you prefer.

proscuitto-wrapped lamb with roasted kipflers

800g (1½ pounds) kipfler (fingerling) potatoes, halved lengthways

400g (12½ ounces) lamb backstrap

2 cloves garlic, sliced finely

4 slices prosciutto (60g)

300g (9½ ounces) green beans, trimmed

2 ruby red grapefruit (700g), segmented

½ cup coarsely chopped fresh flat-leaf parsley

60g reduced-fat fetta, crumbled

1 Preheat oven to 220°C/425°F.

2 Place potato in a medium ovenproof dish; roast, uncovered, for 15 minutes.

3 Meanwhile, cut small slits in lamb; fill each slit with a garlic slice. Wrap prosciutto around lamb. Cook lamb in a heated medium frying pan, over high heat, for 1 minute each side. Remove from pan; place on top of potato.

4 Roast lamb and potato, uncovered, for 10 minutes or until cooked as you like.

5 Meanwhile, boil, steam or microwave beans until tender. Combine beans with remaining ingredients in a medium bowl.

6 Slice lamb; serve with potato and salad.

prep + cook time 45 minutes **serves** 4

cumin fish with roasted corn salsa

4 trimmed corn cobs (1kg)

½ cup coarsely chopped fresh coriander

1 medium red capsicum (200g), chopped finely

6 green onions (scallions), chopped finely

¼ cup (60ml) lime juice

600g (1¼ pounds) firm white fish fillets

2 teaspoons ground cumin

lime or lemon wedges, for serving

1 Cut kernels from corn cobs; roast corn in a heated medium frying pan, stirring constantly. Transfer to a medium bowl. Stir in coriander, capsicum, onion and juice.

2 Sprinkle fish with cumin; cook in the same heated pan.

3 Serve corn salsa topped with fish; accompany with wedges.

prep + cook time 20 minutes **serves** 4

serving suggestion Serve each with a slice of toasted sourdough; this will add an extra 309kJ (73 cal) per serve.

tip Any firm white fish can be used in this recipe.

Check for any small bones in the fillets and use tweezers to remove them.

nutritional count per serving

▶ 8.9g total fat   ▶ 7.9g carbohydrate
▶ 3.4g saturated fat   ▶ 27.1g protein
▶ 949kJ (227 cal)   ▶ 2.9g fibre

tips Patties can be made up to 2 days ahead; cover, refrigerate. Alternatively, freeze for up to 3 months. Fresh baby beetroot can be used instead of canned: wrap in foil and bake in a preheated 180°C/350°F oven for 40 minutes or until tender; cool, then peel.

beef rissoles with beetroot salad

440g (14 ounces) lean minced (ground) beef

1 clove garlic, crushed

1 tablespoon ground cumin

cooking-oil spray

425g (13½ ounces) canned baby beets, drained, halved

⅔ cup coarsely chopped fresh flat-leaf parsley

6 green onions (scallions), sliced thinly

2 tablespoons balsamic vinegar

⅓ cup (65g) low-fat cottage cheese

1 Combine beef, garlic and cumin in a small bowl; shape mixture into eight even-sized patties.

2 Spray a medium heated frying pan with oil; cook patties, over medium heat, for 5 minutes each side or until cooked through.

3 Meanwhile, combine beetroot, parsley, onion and vinegar in a medium bowl.

4 Serve patties with salad; dollop with cheese.

prep + cook time 20 minutes **serves** 4

serving suggestion Serve with a slice of toasted sourdough; this will add an extra 309kJ (73 cal) per serve.

nutritional count per serving

▶ 2.4g total fat   ▶ 42.5g carbohydrate
▶ 0.5g saturated fat   ▶ 33.1g protein
▶ 1422kJ (340 cal)   ▶ 6.2g fibre

tips Have everything prepared before you start to cook. If you like, use brown rice instead of white. For an even quicker cooking time, use a packet of microwave rice as a time-saving shortcut.

honey lemon prawn stir-fry

⅔ cup (130g) white long-grain rice

2 teaspoons sesame seeds

1kg (2 pounds) uncooked king prawns, shelled, deveined, tails intact

2 medium brown onions (150g), halved, cut into wedges

600g (1¼-pound) wombok (napa cabbage), sliced thinly

1 medium carrot (120g), cut into matchsticks

⅓ cup (80ml) lemon juice

2 tablespoons honey

4cm (1½-inch) piece fresh ginger (20g), grated

3 green onions (scallions), sliced thinly

1 Cook rice in a medium saucepan of boiling water until tender; drain.

2 Meanwhile, toast sesame seeds in a heated wok until golden in colour. Transfer to a small bowl.

3 Stir-fry prawns in a heated wok, over high heat, for 5 minutes or until changed in colour and cooked through. Remove from wok; cover to keep warm.

4 Stir-fry brown onion in same wok for 3 minutes or until tender. Return prawns to wok with wombok, carrot, juice, honey and ginger; stir-fry for 2 minutes or until hot.

5 Accompany stir-fry with rice; sprinkle with sesame seeds and green onion to serve.

prep + cook time 25 minutes **serves** 4

tips We used ling for this recipe, but use any firm white fish fillets you like. Fish cakes can be made a day ahead; store, covered, in the fridge.

thai-style fish cakes with cucumber chilli pickle

250g (8 ounces) rice vermicelli

500g (1 pound) firm white fish fillets, chopped coarsely

1 cup loosely packed fresh coriander leaves (cilantro)

⅓ cup (50g) cornflour (cornstarch)

1 tablespoon fish sauce

2 tablespoons sweet chilli sauce

2 egg whites, beaten lightly

3 green onions (scallions), sliced thinly

60g (2 ounce) green beans, trimmed, sliced thinly

120g (4 ounces) baby asian salad mix

cucumber chilli pickle

⅓ cup (80ml) white wine vinegar

1 tablespoon caster (superfine) sugar

2 cloves garlic, crushed

1 fresh small red thai (serrano) chilli, chopped finely

⅓ teaspoon sea salt flakes

2 lebanese cucumbers (260g), halved lengthways, sliced thinly

2 purple shallots (50g), sliced thinly

⅓ cup firmly packed fresh coriander leaves (cilantro)

1 Place vermicelli in a large heatproof bowl, cover with boiling water; stand until tender, drain. Using kitchen scissors, cut vermicelli coarsely.

2 Make cucumber chilli pickle. Combine pickle with half the vermicelli in a medium bowl; season to taste.

3 Process fish until almost smooth. Add coriander, cornflour, sauces and egg white; process until combined. Stir in onion, beans and the remaining vermicelli; season. Shape mixture into 12 patties.

4 Heat a medium non-stick frying pan over medium heat; cook patties for 3 minutes each side or until browned and cooked through. Serve fish cakes with asian salad mix and combined noodles and cucumber chilli pickle.

cucumber chilli pickle Combine vinegar, sugar, garlic, chilli and salt in a medium bowl; stir until sugar dissolves. Add cucumber, shallot and coriander; toss gently to combine.

prep + cook time 40 minutes serves 4

tip To save time, buy char-grilled eggplant and capsicum from the deli section at supermarkets. Drain them well on kitchen paper to remove as much oil as possible.

lentil patties with spicy eggplant sauce

1 small red capsicum (bell pepper) (150g)

1 large potato (300g), chopped coarsely

½ cup (100g) dried red lentils

1 teaspoon olive oil

1 small brown onion (80g), chopped finely

1 clove garlic, crushed

1 tablespoon water

1 stalk celery (150g), trimmed, chopped finely

2 trimmed medium silver beet (swiss chard) leaves (80g), shredded

2 tablespoons roasted pine nuts, chopped coarsely

1 cup (70g) stale wholemeal breadcrumbs

2 teaspoons coarsely chopped fresh coriander (cilantro)

2 teaspoons coarsely chopped fresh flat-leaf parsley

⅓ cup (35g) packaged breadcrumbs, approximately

2 teaspoons vegetable oil

spicy eggplant sauce

1 medium eggplant (300g)

1 clove garlic, crushed

1½ tablespoons lemon juice

2 teaspoons sweet chilli sauce

2 tablespoons low-fat natural yoghurt

1 tablespoon coarsely chopped fresh flat-leaf parsley

1 Make spicy eggplant sauce.

2 Meanwhile, place capsicum on an oven tray. Roast in oven with eggplant for about 30 minutes or until the skin is blackened and blistered. Cover capsicum with plastic or paper for 10 minutes; peel away skin, discard seeds and membranes, then chop flesh coarsely.

3 Meanwhile, boil, steam or microwave potato until tender; drain. Mash potato until smooth.

4 Cook lentils in a medium saucepan of boiling water for about 8 minutes or until tender; drain.

5 Heat olive oil in a medium frying pan over medium heat; cook onion and garlic, stirring, for 5 minutes or until softened. Add the water and celery; cook, stirring, until water has almost evaporated. Add silver beet; cook, stirring, until wilted.

6 Combine mashed potato, lentils, capsicum, onion mixture, pine nuts, stale breadcrumbs and herbs in a large bowl. Shape mixture into 8 patties; toss in packaged breadcrumbs. Place patties on a tray; cover, refrigerate 1 hour.

7 Heat vegetable oil in a large frying pan; cook patties about 2 minutes each side or until browned and heated through. Serve patties with spicy eggplant sauce.

spicy eggplant sauce Preheat oven to 180°C/350°F. Halve eggplant lengthways, place cut-side down on an oiled oven tray. Roast about 45 minutes or until eggplant softens; cool. Scoop out flesh, discard skin. Blend or process eggplant with garlic, juice, sauce and yoghurt until combined. Stir in parsley.

prep + cook time 1½ hours (+ refrigeration) **serves** 4

serving suggestion Serve with a green salad.

tips Use any shaped pasta you like. You can add some finely chopped or grated carrot and zucchini to bulk up the vegetable component of this dish.

chicken, lentil and spinach pasta

2 teaspoons olive oil

1 small brown onion (80g), chopped finely

2 cloves garlic, crushed

150g (4½ ounces) lean minced (ground) chicken

½ cup (100g) dried red lentils

2 cups (500ml) salt-reduced chicken stock

¾ cup (180ml) water

2 tablespoons tomato paste

250g (8 ounces) baby spinach leaves

300g (9½ ounces) pasta shells

1 Heat oil in a medium saucepan over medium heat; cook onion and garlic, stirring, for 5 minutes or until onion softens. Add chicken; cook, stirring, until browned. Stir in lentils, stock, the water and paste; bring to the boil. Reduce heat; simmer, uncovered, about 10 minutes or until lentils are tender. Add spinach; stir until wilted.

2 Meanwhile, cook pasta in a large saucepan of boiling water until just tender; drain.

3 Combine pasta and chicken sauce in a large bowl.

prep + cook time 35 minutes **serves** 4

nutritional count per serving

▶ 8.8g total fat   ▶ 27.4g carbohydrate
▶ 3.3g saturated fat   ▶ 26.1g protein
▶ 1258kJ (301 cal)   ▶ 3.8g fibre

tips You need a small iceberg lettuce for this recipe. You can cook the tortillas following the directions on the packet. Add a small chopped avocado to the salsa to increase the kilojoules; this will add an extra 301kJ (72 cal) to each serving.

beef fajitas

300g (9½ ounces) beef rump steak

8 x 16cm (6-inch) flour tortillas

1 small red capsicum (bell pepper) (150g), sliced thinly

1 small green capsicum (bell pepper) (150g), sliced thinly

1 small yellow capsicum (bell pepper) (150g), sliced thinly

1 medium red onion (170g), sliced thinly

1½ cups finely shredded iceberg lettuce

½ cup (60g) coarsely grated reduced-fat cheddar

fresh tomato salsa

1 large tomato (220g), seeded, chopped finely

1 small red onion (100g), chopped finely

2 teaspoons finely chopped drained jalapeño chillies

2 tablespoons finely chopped fresh coriander (cilantro)

2 teaspoons lemon juice

1 Make fresh tomato salsa.

2 Cook beef on a heated oiled grill plate (or grill or barbecue) for about 3 minutes both sides or until cooked as desired. Cover beef; rest 10 minutes, then slice thinly.

3 Preheat grill (broiler); cover tortillas with foil; place under grill until warmed through or, cover with kitchen paper and warm in a microwave oven.

4 Meanwhile, cook capsicum and onion on same grill plate until vegetables are tender.

5 Divide beef, capsicum and onion among tortillas. Top with lettuce, cheese and fresh tomato salsa; roll to enclose filling.

fresh tomato salsa Combine ingredients in a medium bowl; season to taste.

prep + cook time 50 minutes **serves** 4

warm pasta and lamb salad

500g (1 pound) lamb fillets

⅓ cup (80ml) lemon juice

2 tablespoons finely chopped fresh rosemary

1 tablespoon dry red wine

1 tablespoon sweet chilli sauce

1 teaspoon brown sugar

1 clove garlic, crushed

1 tablespoon olive oil

4 medium roma (egg) tomatoes (300g), quartered

350g (11 ounces) wholemeal spiral pasta

½ cup (125ml) salt-reduced beef stock

2 tablespoons coarsely chopped fresh flat-leaf parsley

500g (1 pound) spinach, trimmed, chopped coarsely

1 Combine lamb, juice, rosemary, wine, sauce, sugar, garlic and half the oil in a medium bowl. Cover, refrigerate 2 hours.

2 Preheat oven to 180°C/350°F.

3 Lightly oil oven tray. Place tomato, in a single layer, on tray. Bake about 20 minutes or until soft.

4 Cook pasta in a large saucepan of boiling water until just tender; drain.

5 Meanwhile, drain lamb over a medium bowl; reserve marinade. Heat remaining oil in a medium frying pan over medium heat; cook lamb for about 4 minutes or until browned and cooked as desired. Cover lamb; rest for 5 minutes, then slice thinly.

6 Add reserved marinade, stock and parsley to the same pan; bring to the boil.

7 Combine tomato, pasta, lamb, marinade mixture and spinach in a large bowl; season to taste.

prep + cook time 50 minutes (+ refrigeration) **serves** 4

tips Substitute the lamb with chicken breast, if you prefer. Use any shape wholemeal pasta you like.

Serve the stir-fry with steamed rice or rice noodles.

tips Swap beef for lamb, if you like. Beef can be marinated with spices a day ahead; store, covered, in the fridge. You could also swap the sugar snap peas with snow peas.

five-spice beef and asian greens

300g (9½ ounces) beef fillet, sliced thinly

2cm (¾-inch) piece fresh ginger (10g), grated

1 teaspoon chinese five-spice powder

1 teaspoon peanut oil

¼ cup (60ml) dark soy sauce

2 tablespoons water

2 tablespoons honey

2 teaspoons lemon juice

500g (1 pound) gai lan, trimmed, quartered crossways

350g (11 ounces) choy sum, trimmed, quartered crossways

150g (4½ ounces) sugar snap peas, trimmed

½ teaspoon sesame seeds

1 Combine beef, ginger and five-spice in a small bowl.

2 Heat oil in a wok; stir-fry beef until browned. Remove beef from wok.

3 Add sauce, the water, honey and juice to wok; bring to the boil. Reduce heat; simmer for 2 minutes.

4 Return beef to wok with vegetables; stir-fry until gai lan is tender. Serve sprinkled with seeds.

prep + cook time 20 minutes **serves** 4

tips Swap the pork mince for a pork and veal mince mixture, if you like. Patties can be made a day ahead; store, covered, in the fridge, or freeze for up to 3 months. Add 2 teaspoons of olive oil to the pan before cooking patties, if you like; this will add an extra 84kJ (20 cal) to each serving.

pork rissoles with peppered greens

600g (1¼ pounds) lean minced (ground) pork

2 cloves garlic, crushed

1 medium brown onion (150g), chopped finely

½ cup coarsely chopped fresh mint

2 egg whites, beaten lightly

⅔ cup (50g) stale breadcrumbs

12 medium silver beet (swiss chard) leaves (780g), trimmed, shredded coarsely

4 cups (320g) finely shredded savoy cabbage

200g (6½ ounces) baby spinach leaves

½ teaspoon cracked black pepper

3 teaspoons dijon mustard

1 tablespoon plain (all-purpose) flour

1 cup (250ml) chicken stock

1 cup (250ml) dry white wine

1 Combine pork, half the garlic, and all the onion, mint, egg white and breadcrumbs in a medium bowl; season. Shape mixture into 12 patties; place on tray. Cover; refrigerate for 30 minutes.

2 Heat a large non-stick frying pan over medium heat; cook silver beet, cabbage, spinach, pepper and remaining garlic, stirring, for 5 minutes or until greens wilt. Season to taste. Remove from pan; cover to keep warm.

3 Cook patties in same pan until browned both sides and cooked through. Remove from pan; cover to keep warm.

4 Add mustard, flour, stock and wine to pan; cook, stirring, until mixture boils and thickens. Strain sauce into a small heatproof jug. Serve rissoles with greens and sauce.

prep + cook time 45 minutes (+ refrigeration)   **serves** 4

Cook the rice a day ahead: spread in a thin layer on a tray to cool, then cover and place in the refrigerator.

tip You could swap the green beans with peas, if you like.

brown fried rice with omelette

1⅓ cups (265g) brown long-grain rice

1 tablespoon peanut oil

3 eggs, beaten lightly

2 cloves garlic, crushed

3cm (1¼-inch) piece fresh ginger (15g), grated finely

1 fresh long red chilli, chopped finely

1 small red capsicum (bell pepper) (150g), cut into 1cm (½-inch) pieces

115g (3½ ounces) baby corn, cut into 1cm (½-inch) pieces

100g (3 ounces) green beans, trimmed, cut into 1cm (½-inch) pieces

100g (3 ounces) fresh shiitake mushrooms, sliced thinly

2 tablespoons salt-reduced soy sauce

2 tablespoons rice vinegar

½ cup (40g) bean sprouts, trimmed

4 green onions (scallions), sliced thinly

1 Cook rice in a large saucepan of boiling water until tender; drain. Cool completely.

2 Heat half the oil in a wok; pour in half the egg, tilt wok to coat with egg. Cook until omelette is set. Remove omelette; roll tightly. Repeat with remaining egg. Slice omelettes thinly.

3 Heat remaining oil in wok; stir-fry garlic, ginger and chilli until fragrant. Add capsicum, corn, beans and mushrooms to wok; stir-fry until tender.

4 Add rice, sauce, vinegar and sprouts; stir-fry until hot. Stir in half the onion.

5 Serve rice topped with remaining onion and omelette strips.

prep + cook time 45 minutes (+ cooling) **serves** 4

nutritional count per serving

▶ 2g total fat
▶ 0.6g saturated fat
▶ 610kJ (146 cal)

▶ 9.8g carbohydrate
▶ 19.2g protein
▶ 4.1g fibre

tips Swap the red cabbage with white cabbage or wombok (napa cabbage). The pork can be marinated a day ahead; store, covered, in the fridge. Add 2 tablespoons pine nuts to the asian coleslaw for added crunch; this will add an extra 211kJ (50 cal) per serve.

pork with asian coleslaw

2 tablespoons light soy sauce

1 tablespoon brown sugar

1 tablespoon mirin

1 clove garlic, crushed

300g (9½ ounces) pork fillet

cooking-oil spray

asian coleslaw

3 cups (240g) finely shredded red cabbage

1 large carrot (180g), cut into thin matchsticks

4 green onions (scallions), sliced thinly

¼ cup firmly packed fresh coriander leaves (cilantro)

1 tablespoon light soy sauce

2 teaspoons brown sugar

2 teaspoons lemon juice

1 Combine sauce, sugar, mirin, garlic and pork in a medium bowl. Cover; refrigerate 1 hour.
2 Make asian coleslaw.
3 Spray heated barbecue plate (or grill or grill plate) with oil; cook pork, turning occasionally, for 8 minutes or until browned all over and cooked as desired. Cover pork; rest for 5 minutes, then slice thinly. Serve pork with coleslaw.
asian coleslaw Combine ingredients in a large bowl.

prep + cook time 20 minutes (+ refrigeration) **serves** 4

Chicken breast fillets can be used instead of the pork, if you prefer.

healthy salads

roasted mediterranean tomato salad

Preheat oven to 240°C/475°F. Halve 1 small red and 1 small green tomato; combine with 100g cherry tomatoes, 80g each red and yellow teardrop tomatoes and 1⅓ tablespoons olive oil in a large shallow baking dish. Roast, uncovered, 10 minutes. Remove from oven; cool 30 minutes. Combine tomato mixture with 1½ tablespoons balsamic vinegar, 1 tablespoon fresh small basil leaves and 2 teaspoons each of fresh oregano and thyme leaves in a large bowl. Serve with grissini (breadsticks), if you like.

prep + cook time 20 minutes (+ cooling) **serves** 4
nutritional count per serving 3.8g total fat (0.5g saturated fat); 209kJ (50 cal); 2.4g carbohydrate; 1g protein; 1.6g fibre

three-bean salad with lemon chilli crumbs

To make chilli breadcrumbs, melt 15g (½ ounce) butter in a small frying pan; cook 3 teaspoons finely grated lemon rind, 2½ tablespoons stale breadcrumbs and ¼ teaspoon chilli powder over low heat, stirring, until crumbs are browned. Boil, steam or microwave 50g (1½ ounces) each green and yellow beans and 200g (6½ ounces) broad beans, separately, until tender; drain. Rinse under cold water; drain. Peel away grey outer shells from broad beans. Place all beans in a medium bowl with 1 tablespoon olive oil and 1 tablespoon lemon juice; toss gently to combine. Serve sprinkled with breadcrumbs.

prep + cook time 25 minutes **serves** 4
nutritional count per serving 10g total fat (3.2g saturated fat); 594kJ (142 cal); 5.3g carbohydrate; 5.2g protein; 4.8g fibre

borlotti bean, brown rice and almond salad

Place 1 cup dried borlotti beans in a small bowl, cover with water; stand overnight, drain. Rinse under cold water; drain. Cook beans in a small saucepan of boiling water, uncovered; until just tender; drain. Rinse under cold water; drain. Meanwhile, cook 1 cup brown long-grain rice in a small saucepan of boiling water until tender; drain. Rinse under cold water; drain. Place beans and rice in a medium bowl with 1 finely chopped small red onion, 1 cup each of finely chopped fresh flat-leaf parsley and mint, 3 finely chopped medium tomatoes, 2 tablespoons roasted slivered almonds, ¼ cup lemon juice and 1 tablespoon olive oil; toss gently to combine.

prep + cook time 45 minutes (+ standing) **serves** 4
nutritional count per serving 10.6g total fat (1.3g saturated fat); 1584kJ (379 cal); 61.3g carbohydrate; 18.7g protein; 16.3g fibre

rocket, parmesan and semi-dried tomato salad

Combine 100g (3 ounces) baby rocket leaves (arugula), 2 tablespoons pine nuts, 40g (1½ ounces) drained coarsely chopped semi-dried tomato and ⅓ cup shaved parmesan in a large bowl. Combine 1 tablespoon olive oil and 1 tablespoon balsamic vinegar; toss through salad to combine.

prep time 10 minutes **serves** 4
nutritional count per serving 12.3g total fat (2.3g saturated fat); 635kJ (152 cal); 4.4g carbohydrate; 5.1g protein; 2.2g fibre

herbed ricotta ravioli with tomato salsa

500g (1 pound) spinach, trimmed

⅓ cup (80g) reduced-fat ricotta

1 egg white

1 tablespoon finely chopped fresh basil

2 teaspoons finely chopped fresh mint

1 teaspoon finely chopped fresh rosemary

24 wonton wrappers

tomato salsa

4 large roma (egg) tomatoes (360g), chopped finely

¼ cup loosely packed fresh baby basil leaves

1 tablespoon white balsamic vinegar

½ teaspoon olive oil

1 Boil, steam or microwave spinach until wilted; rinse under cold water, drain. When cool enough to handle, squeeze excess liquid from spinach; shred spinach finely.

2 Combine ricotta, egg white, herbs and spinach in a medium bowl. Divide spinach mixture among half the wonton wrappers; brush edges with a little water. Top with remaining wrappers, press around edges firmly to seal.

3 Place four ravioli in a large baking-paper-lined bamboo steamer; cook over a large saucepan of simmering water for 5 minutes or until cooked through. Cover to keep warm. Repeat until all ravioli are cooked.

4 Meanwhile, make tomato salsa. Serve ravioli topped with tomato salsa.

tomato salsa Combine ingredients in a small bowl; season.

prep + cook time 35 minutes **serves** 4

tip Ravioli can be made a day ahead; place on a baking-paper-lined tray in a single layer, cover with plastic wrap and refrigerate.

grilled pepper lamb with roasted vegetables

1 large kumara (orange sweet potato) (500g), unpeeled, sliced thinly

8 shallots (200g), quartered

2 large red capsicums (bell pepper) (700g), sliced thickly

4 flat mushrooms (320g), quartered

4 stalks fresh rosemary

1 cup (160g) pitted green olives

cooking-oil spray

340g (11 ounces) asparagus, halved

600g (1¼ pounds) lamb fillets

2 teaspoons cracked black pepper

2 tablespoons lemon juice

⅔ cup loosely packed fresh flat-leaf parsley leaves

⅔ cup loosely packed fresh mint leaves

lemon cheeks or wedges, to serve

1 Preheat oven to 200°C/400°F.

2 Combine kumara, shallot, capsicum, mushrooms, rosemary and olives in a large baking dish. Spray with oil; season, mix gently. Roast, uncovered, for 35 minutes or until vegetables are tender, adding asparagus to the dish for the last 15 minutes of cooking time. Discard rosemary.

3 Meanwhile, combine lamb and pepper in a small bowl. Cook lamb on a heated oiled grill plate (or grill or barbecue) for about 5 minutes, turning occasionally, until browned all over and cooked as desired. Cover lamb; rest for 5 minutes, then slice thickly.

4 Stir juice and herbs into vegetable mixture. Serve lamb with vegetables; accompany with lemon cheeks.

prep + cook time 55 minutes **serves** 4

tip To use preserved lemon rind, wash the lemon well to remove salt; discard the flesh, and finely chop the rind.

spice-rubbed beef with chickpea salad

1 teaspoon each of coriander seeds, dried chilli flakes and sea salt

2 cloves garlic, crushed

600g (1¼-pound) piece beef eye fillet, trimmed

6 large roma (egg) tomatoes (540g), peeled

400g (12½ ounces) canned chickpeas (garbanzo beans), rinsed, drained

2 tablespoons finely chopped preserved lemon rind

1 cup finely chopped fresh flat-leaf parsley

1 cup loosely packed fresh coriander leaves (cilantro)

1 tablespoon lemon juice

cooking-oil spray

120g (4 ounces) baby spinach leaves

1 Using a mortar and pestle, crush seeds, chilli flakes, salt and garlic into a coarse paste; rub paste onto beef. Cover; refrigerate 20 minutes.

2 Preheat oven to 200°C/400°F. Line oven tray with baking paper.

3 Meanwhile, quarter tomatoes; discard seeds and pulp. Chop tomato flesh finely. Place in a medium bowl with chickpeas, rind, herbs and juice; toss gently to combine.

4 Lightly spray a heated grill plate (or grill or barbecue) with oil; cook beef until browned all over. Transfer to an oven tray; cook, uncovered, in oven, for 20 minutes (for medium) or until cooked as you like.

5 Cover beef; rest for 10 minutes, then slice thinly. Serve with chickpea salad; accompany with spinach.

prep + cook time 45 minutes (+ refrigeration) **serves** 4

chermoulla lamb with chickpea salad

400g (12½ ounces) lamb backstrap

2 large pitta breads (160g)

420g (13½ ounces) canned chickpeas (garbanzo beans), rinsed, drained

1 small red onion (100g), sliced thinly

4 medium tomatoes (600g), cut into thin wedges

⅓ cup each fresh mint and coriander leaves (cilantro)

120g (4 ounces) baby rocket leaves (arugula), shredded coarsely

⅓ cup (80ml) lemon juice

⅔ cup (190g) skim-milk yoghurt

lemon wedges, to serve

chermoulla

1½ cups coarsely chopped fresh coriander (cilantro)

1 cup coarsely chopped fresh flat-leaf parsley

2 cloves garlic, crushed

2 teaspoons each of ground cumin and paprika

⅓ cup (80ml) lemon juice

⅓ cup (80ml) water

1 Make chermoulla. Reserve half the chermoulla. Combine remaining chermoulla and lamb in a medium bowl; season.

2 Cook lamb and bread on a heated oiled grill plate (or grill or barbecue) until lamb is cooked as desired and bread is crisp. Cover lamb; rest for 5 minutes, then slice thinly. Break bread into pieces.

3 Meanwhile to make salad, combine chickpeas, onion, tomato, herbs, rocket and juice in a medium bowl; season to taste.

4 Divide salad between serving plates, top with lamb and reserved chermoulla. Accompany with bread, yoghurt and lemon wedges.

chermoulla Blend or process ingredients until smooth.

prep + cook time 45 minutes serves 4

tips Substitute lamb with chicken breast, if you like. Chermoulla is a marinade of fresh and ground herbs and spices often used in the cooking of North Africa

This is a good dish to double the recipe and freeze half for later.

mushroom beef and barley casserole

2 tablespoons olive oil

1kg (2 pounds) beef chuck steak, diced into 3cm (1¼-inch) cubes

8 pickling onions (320g), halved

2 medium carrots (240g), chopped coarsely

1 cup (250ml) dry red wine

1 cup (250ml) beef stock

800g (1½ pounds) canned diced tomatoes

2 stalks fresh rosemary

7 black peppercorns

200g (6½ ounces) button mushrooms

½ cup (100g) pearl barley

2 tablespoons fresh oregano leaves

1 Preheat oven to 180°C/350°F.

2 Heat half the oil in a large flameproof casserole dish on the stove top; cook beef, in batches, over high heat, until browned. Remove from pan.

3 Heat remaining oil in same dish; cook onion and carrot, stirring, until vegetables soften. Return beef to dish with wine, stock, tomatoes, rosemary and peppercorns; bring to the boil. Cover, transfer dish to oven; cook for 2 hours, stirring occasionally.

4 Stir mushrooms and barley into dish; return uncovered dish to oven. Cook casserole for 45 minutes or until barley is tender. Serve sprinkled with oregano.

prep + cook time 3¼ hours **serves** 4

tip To save time, ask the butcher to dice the meat for you.

tip Scrub potatoes under cold running water to remove any dirt. Kipfler potatoes can be swapped for any variety of potatoes suitable for baking, such as pontiac, bintje, desiree or sebago.

herb-stuffed chicken with tomato salad

600g (1¼ pounds) kipfler (fingerling) potatoes, unpeeled

cooking-oil spray

¼ cup finely chopped fresh basil

1 tablespoon finely chopped fresh oregano

2 teaspoons fresh lemon thyme

2 cloves garlic, crushed

1 tablespoon finely grated lemon rind

4 x 150g (4½ ounces) chicken breast fillets

4 slices prosciutto (60g)

tomato salad

250g (8 ounces) red cherry tomatoes

250g (8 ounces) yellow cherry tomatoes

150g (4½ ounces) baby spinach leaves

½ cup coarsely chopped fresh basil

2 tablespoons red wine vinegar

2 teaspoons olive oil

1 Preheat oven to 220°C/425°F. Oil a large baking dish.

2 Halve unpeeled potatoes lengthways. Place potato, in a single layer, in dish; spray lightly with oil. Roast for about 45 minutes or until browned lightly and tender.

3 Meanwhile, combine finely chopped basil, oregano, thyme, garlic and rind in a small bowl. Halve chicken breasts horizontally, without cutting all the way through; open chicken breasts out flat. Divide herb mixture among chicken pieces; fold to enclose filling, wrapping each with a prosciutto slice to secure.

4 Cook chicken in a heated oiled large frying pan until browned all over; place chicken on an oven tray. Roast in oven during the last 15 minutes of the potato cooking time, or until chicken is cooked through.

5 Meanwhile, make tomato salad. Serve salad with chicken and potatoes; sprinkle over extra lemon thyme leaves, if you like.

tomato salad Cook tomatoes in a heated oiled large frying pan, stirring, over high heat, for 3 minutes. Combine tomatoes, spinach and basil in a large bowl with the combined vinegar and oil.

prep + cook time 1¼ hours **serves** 4

prawn and basil risotto

½ cup (100g) brown long-grain rice

500g (1 pound) uncooked medium king prawns (shrimp)

1 cup (250ml) salt-reduced chicken stock

1 cup (250ml) dry white wine

3 cups (750ml) water

1 stalk celery (150g), trimmed, chopped finely

1 small brown onion (80g), chopped finely

1 cup (200g) arborio rice

2 medium tomatoes (300g), seeded, chopped finely

½ cup loosely packed fresh basil leaves

2 tablespoons finely chopped fresh flat-leaf parsley

1 Cook brown rice according to packet directions.

2 Shell and devein prawns, leaving tails intact.

3 Bring stock, wine and 2 cups of the water to the boil in a medium saucepan. Reduce heat; simmer, covered.

4 Meanwhile, cook celery, onion and the remaining water in a large saucepan, stirring, for 10 minutes or until water has evaporated. Stir in arborio rice.

5 Add ½ cup of the simmering stock mixture to the rice mixture; cook, stirring, over low heat, until liquid is absorbed. Continue adding stock mixture, in ½-cup batches, stirring until liquid is absorbed after each addition. Total cooking time should be about 35 minutes or until rice is tender.

6 After last addition of stock mixture, add prawns and brown rice; cook, stirring, until prawns are changed in colour. Remove from heat; stir in tomato and herbs.

prep + cook time 50 minutes **serves** 4

lemon-chilli pork with italian brown rice salad

2 teaspoons finely grated lemon rind

2 tablespoons lemon juice

½ teaspoon dried chilli flakes

2 teaspoons olive oil

4 x 240g (7½-ounce) pork cutlets

italian brown rice salad

1 cup (200g) brown long-grain rice

1 medium red capsicum (bell pepper) (200g), chopped finely

½ cup (60g) pitted black olives, chopped coarsely

2 tablespoons rinsed, drained capers

½ cup coarsely chopped fresh basil

⅓ cup coarsely chopped fresh flat-leaf parsley

2 tablespoons lemon juice

2 teaspoons olive oil

1 Combine rind, juice, chilli, oil and pork in a medium bowl. Cover, refrigerate for 2 hours.
2 Meanwhile, make italian brown rice salad.
3 Cook pork on a heated oiled grill plate (or grill or barbecue), over medium heat, for 4 minutes each side or until browned and cooked as desired. Cover pork; rest for 5 minutes. Serve with rice salad.

italian brown rice salad Cook rice in a large saucepan of boiling water until tender; drain. Rinse under cold water; drain. Combine rice and remaining ingredients in a large bowl; season to taste.

prep + cook time 50 minutes (+ refrigeration) **serves** 4

serving suggestion Accompany with a rocket (arugula) or spinach salad.

tip Pork can be marinated and frozen for up to 3 months. Defrost in the refrigerator overnight before cooking.

Use Golden Delicious apples – a crisp almost citrus-coloured apple – if you prefer. They have an excellent flavour and hold their shape during cooking.

tip A flameproof baking dish can be cast iron, a heavy-based roasting pan or a heatproof crockery dish.

quick roast pork with apple and sage onions

1 tablespoon olive oil

500g (1 pound) lean pork fillet

2 tablespoons dijon mustard

2 tablespoons finely chopped fresh flat-leaf parsley

2 tablespoons honey

2 large red apples (400g), unpeeled, cut into 5mm (¼-inch) rounds

1 large red onion (300g), cut into thin wedges

16 sage leaves

2 tablespoons plain (all-purpose) flour

2 cups (500ml) salt-reduced chicken stock

300g (9½ ounces) green beans, trimmed

1 Preheat oven to 200°C/400°F.

2 Heat half the oil in a medium flameproof baking dish on the stove top over high heat; cook pork until browned all over. Remove from heat. Combine mustard, parsley and honey in a small bowl; brush mustard mixture all over pork, season.

3 Place apple, onion and sage around pork in dish; drizzle with remaining oil. Transfer to oven; roast, uncovered, for 20 minutes or until pork is cooked through. Remove pork, apples, onion and sage from dish, cover with foil; stand 10 minutes.

4 Place dish over medium heat on stove top. Add flour; cook, stirring, until mixture thickens and bubbles. Gradually add stock; cook, stirring, until gravy boils and thickens slightly, season.

5 Meanwhile, boil, steam or microwave beans until tender; drain.

6 Serve sliced pork with baked apples, onions and sage, gravy and beans.

prep + cook time 45 minutes **serves** 4

Use a vegetable peeler to
slice the zucchini lengthways
into thin ribbons.

nutritional count per serving

▶ 8g total fat   ▶ 41.3g carbohydrate
▶ 2.6g saturated fat   ▶ 24g protein
▶ 1480kJ (354 cal)   ▶ 8.1g fibre

lamb cutlets with parsnip mash and zucchini salad

4 medium potatoes (800g), chopped coarsely

2 large parsnips (700g), chopped coarsely

1 cup (250ml) skim milk, warmed

2 teaspoons olive oil

2 teaspoons finely grated lemon rind

¼ cup (60ml) lemon juice

2 tablespoons flaked parmesan

2 large green zucchini (300g), cut into ribbons

2 large yellow zucchini (300g), cut into ribbons

80g (2½ ounces) baby rocket leaves (arugula)

8 french-trimmed lamb cutlets (400g)

1 Boil, steam or microwave potato and parsnip until tender; drain. Mash potato and parsnip with milk in a large bowl until smooth; season to taste. Cover to keep warm.

2 Meanwhile, combine oil, rind and juice in a medium bowl; add cheese, zucchini and rocket, mix gently. Stand 15 minutes; season to taste.

3 Cook lamb on a heated oiled grill plate (or grill or barbecue) for 3 minutes each side or until cooked as desired.

4 Serve lamb with mash and zucchini salad.

prep + cook time 45 minutes (+ standing) **serves** 4

tips You could buy 4 x 75g (2½-ounce) salmon fillets instead of the larger fillet. The yellow beans add some colour to the dish; if unavailable use green beans.

roasted salmon and warm potato salad

16 kipfler (fingerling) potatoes (800g), unpeeled, halved

cooking-oil spray

300g (9½-ounce) salmon fillet, skin and bones removed

⅓ cup (80ml) buttermilk

1 tablespoon lemon juice

1 tablespoon dijon mustard

2 well-drained anchovy fillets, chopped finely

4 gherkins (80g), chopped finely

⅓ cup (80ml) finely chopped fresh flat-leaf parsley

2 cloves garlic, crushed

340g (11 ounces) asparagus, trimmed, halved

300g (9½ ounces) snow peas, trimmed, halved

300g (9½ ounces) yellow beans, halved lengthways

2 cups (230g) firmly packed trimmed watercress

1 Preheat oven to 200°C/400°F.

2 Place potato on a baking-paper-lined oven tray; spray potato with oil, season. Roast, uncovered, for 30 minutes. Cut fish into quarters, place on top of potatoes; roast, uncovered, for about 15 minutes or until potato is browned lightly and tender and salmon is cooked as desired.

3 Meanwhile, combine buttermilk, juice, mustard, anchovy, gherkin, parsley and garlic in a small bowl; season to taste.

4 Boil, steam or microwave asparagus, snow peas and beans, separately, until tender; drain. Rinse under cold water; drain.

5 Combine watercress, potato, asparagus, snow peas, beans and fish on serving plates; drizzle with buttermilk dressing.

prep + cook time 1 hour   **serves** 4

tips Preserved lemons are salted lemons preserved in a mixture of olive oil and lemon juice or water, and are available from specialty food shops and delicatessens. Rinse well before using, and use the rind only (discard the flesh). For a non-vegetarian meal, char-grill and thinly slice a small chicken breast fillet.

grilled zucchini with pumpkin and couscous

½ cup (100g) couscous

½ cup (125ml) boiling water

2 tablespoons lemon juice

2 teaspoons olive oil

¼ cup (40g) pine nuts

1 clove garlic, crushed

½ small red onion (50g), chopped finely

1 teaspoon sweet smoked paprika

½ teaspoon each of ground cumin and cayenne pepper

½ small red capsicum (bell pepper) (75g), chopped finely

200g (6½-ounce) piece pumpkin, chopped finely

2 tablespoons finely chopped fresh flat-leaf parsley

6 medium zucchini (720g), halved lengthways

preserved lemon yoghurt

½ cup (140g) greek-style yoghurt

2 tablespoons finely chopped preserved lemon rind

2 tablespoons water

1 Make preserved lemon yoghurt.

2 Combine couscous with the water and juice in a large heatproof bowl; cover, stand for 5 minutes or until liquid is absorbed, fluffing with a fork occasionally.

3 Heat oil in a large saucepan; cook nuts, stirring, over medium heat until browned lightly. Add garlic, onion and spices; cook, stirring, for 5 minutes or until onion softens. Add capsicum and pumpkin; cook, stirring, until pumpkin is just tender. Stir in couscous and parsley.

4 Meanwhile, cook zucchini on a heated oiled grill plate (or grill or barbecue) until just tender. Serve zucchini topped with couscous and drizzled with yoghurt.

preserved lemon yoghurt Combine ingredients in a small bowl.

prep + cook time 40 minutes **serves** 4

healthy salads

thai herb and mango salad

To make palm sugar and lime dressing, combine ¼ cup lime juice, 1 tablespoon fish sauce, 2 tablespoons grated palm sugar and 2 cloves crushed garlic in a screw-top jar; shake well. Slice cheeks from 2 medium mangoes; cut each cheek into thin strips. Place mango in a large bowl with a thinly sliced 10cm (4-inch) stick fresh lemon grass, 2 thinly sliced fresh long red chillies, 150g (4 ½ ounces) trimmed, thinly sliced snow peas, 6 thinly sliced green onions (scallions), 1 cup bean sprouts, ½ cup loosely packed fresh coriander leaves, ¼ cup each of loosely packed fresh mint and vietnamese mint leaves, 1 tablespoon coarsely shredded thai basil and the dressing; toss gently to combine.

prep time 25 minutes **serves** 4
nutritional count per serving 0.6g total fat (0g saturated fat); 631kJ (151 cal); 29.3g carbohydrate; 4.5g protein; 5g fibre

soba salad with seaweed, ginger and vegetables

Place 20g (¾ ounce) wakame in a small bowl, cover with cold water; stand about 10 minutes or until wakame softens, drain. Discard any hard stems; chop coarsely. Meanwhile, cook 200g (6½ ounces) dried soba noodles in a small saucepan of boiling water until just tender; drain. Rinse under cold water; drain. Chop noodles coarsely. Place wakame and noodles in a medium bowl with 2 seeded lebanese cucumbers, 2 small carrots cut into matchsticks, 1 tablespoon toasted sesame seeds, 3 thinly sliced green onions (scallions), 2cm (¾-inch) piece of grated ginger, 2 teaspoons sesame oil, ¼ cup lime juice and 1 tablespoon tamari; toss gently. Sprinkle with extra sesame seeds to serve.

prep + cook time 30 minutes **serves** 4
nutritional count per serving 4.6g total fat (0.6g saturated fat); 1003kJ (240 cal); 37.5g carbohydrate; 8.1g protein; 6.1g fibre

tip Wakame is a bright-green seaweed, usually sold dried; it's available from most Asian food stores.

blood orange and beetroot salad

To make orange dressing, combine ⅓ cup strained blood orange juice, 1 tablespoon each of lemon juice and olive oil and 2 tablespoons white wine vinegar in a screw-top jar; shake well. Cook 680g (1¼ pounds) trimmed asparagus in a medium saucepan of boiling water for 1 minute; drain, rinse under cold water, drain. Arrange 200g (6½ ounces) curly endive and 250g (8 ounces) red witlof leaves on serving plates; top with 800g (1½ pounds) drained halved canned beetroot, 1 tablespoon toasted pine nuts, asparagus, 4 segmented medium blood oranges and 150g (4½ ounces) low-fat fetta. Drizzle with orange dressing.

prep + cook time 15 minutes **serves** 4
nutritional count per serving 13.2g total fat (4.3g saturated fat); 1427kJ (341 cal); 31.1g carbohydrate; 18.7g protein; 11.6g fibre

tip Blood oranges are available in winter, at other times use navel oranges.

tomato and kumara rice salad

Cook 1 cup brown long-grain rice in a large saucepan of boiling water about 30 minutes or until tender; drain. Rinse under cold water; drain. Boil, steam or microwave 1 coarsely chopped small kumara (orange sweet potato) until tender; drain. Combine 2 tablespoons orange juice, 1 tablespoon white balsamic vinegar and 1 clove crushed garlic in a screw-top jar; shake well. Combine rice, kumara and balsamic dressing in a large bowl with 250g (8 ounces) halved red grape tomatoes, 2 thinly sliced green onions (scallions), ½ cup coarsely chopped fresh basil leaves and 40g (1½ ounces) baby rocket leaves (arugula); toss gently to combine.

prep + cook time 40 minutes **serves** 4
nutritional count per serving 1.5g total fat (0.3g saturated fat); 1021kJ (244 cal); 48.9g carbohydrate; 5.8g protein; 4.5g fibre

tip Substitute white wine vinegar or balsamic vinegar for the white balsamic vinegar, if you like.

dessert weekdays

mango, berry and passionfruit frozen yoghurt

1 small mango (300g)

250g (8 ounces) strawberries

2 cups (560g) low-fat vanilla-flavoured yoghurt

¼ cup (60ml) passionfruit pulp

1 Blend or process half the mango and half the strawberries, separately, until smooth; finely chop remaining mango and berries. Refrigerate berry puree and berries until needed.
2 Combine mango puree, chopped mango and ½ cup of the yoghurt in a medium bowl; divide mango mixture among eight 1-cup (250ml) disposable cups. Cover, freeze for 1 hour or until surface is firm.
3 Combine berry puree, chopped berries and ½ cup of the yoghurt in a medium bowl; divide berry mixture among the cups. Cover, freeze for 1 hour or until surface is firm.
4 Combine passionfruit pulp and remaining yoghurt in a medium bowl; divide passionfruit mixture among cups. Cover, freeze for 1 hour. Press an ice-block stick firmly into the mixture in each cup. Cover, freeze 3 hours or overnight.
5 Remove from cups and serve immediately.

prep time 35 minutes (+ freezing) **makes** 8

tip The recipe needs to be made a day ahead. Frozen yoghurt will keep in the freezer for up to 3 months. Once frozen, store them in an airtight container in the freezer.

nutritional count per serving

▶ 3.3g total fat
▶ 0.3g saturated fat
▶ 1066kJ (255 cal)

▶ 51.2g carbohydrate
▶ 3.2g protein
▶ 7g fibre

blackberry apple crumble

800g (1½ pounds) canned pie apple

1 cup (150g) frozen blackberries

2 tablespoons caster (superfine) sugar

⅔ cup (60g) rolled oats

2 tablespoons pure maple syrup

2 tablespoons flaked almonds

½ teaspoon ground cinnamon

1 Preheat oven to 180°C/350°F. Grease four 1-cup (250ml) ovenproof dishes.

2 Combine apple, blackberries and sugar in a medium bowl; spoon mixture into dishes.

3 Combine oats, syrup, nuts and cinnamon in a small bowl; sprinkle crumble mixture over fruit mixture. Bake, uncovered, for 40 minutes or until heated through and browned lightly.

prep + cook time 50 minutes **serves** 4

tips You can swap the apple and blackberries for canned pears and frozen raspberries. The crumble is best baked just before serving.

Oats are high in fibre and have a low glycaemic index (good for those with diabetes). Use traditional oats rather than quick-cooking oats.

nutritional count per serving

▶ 0.4g total fat
▶ 0g saturated fat
▶ 669kJ (160 cal)

▶ 31.2g carbohydrate
▶ 5.2g protein
▶ 5g fibre

tip The crêpes can be made a day ahead; layer them between sheets of baking paper, then cover and store in the fridge. They can also be frozen for up to 3 months.

crêpes with roasted strawberries

500g (1 pound) strawberries, halved

2 tablespoons caster (superfine) sugar

1 teaspoon vanilla extract

2 small oranges (360g), segmented

½ cup (75g) plain (all-purpose) flour

2 tablespoons skim milk

⅔ cup (160ml) water

2 tablespoons finely shredded fresh mint

1 Preheat oven to 180°C/350°F. Line a shallow baking dish with baking paper.

2 Place strawberries in dish; sprinkle with sugar, then drizzle with extract, turn gently to combine.

3 Roast, uncovered, for 7 minutes or until strawberries start to soften. Remove dish from oven; stir in orange segments.

4 Meanwhile, sift flour into a small bowl; gradually whisk in combined milk and water until batter is smooth.

5 Heat a medium non-stick frying pan over medium heat; pour in a quarter of the batter, tilt pan to cover base with batter. Cook crêpe until browned lightly, loosening edge with a spatula. Turn crêpe; brown other side. Remove crêpe from pan; cover to keep warm. Repeat with remaining batter.

6 Serve crêpes topped with strawberry mixture and mint.

prep + cook time 20 minutes **serves** 4

chocolate fudge cakes

½ cup (50g) cocoa powder

¾ cup (165g) firmly packed brown sugar

½ cup (125ml) boiling water

75g (2½ ounces) dark (semi-sweet) chocolate, chopped finely

2 egg yolks

¼ cup (25g) ground hazelnuts

⅓ cup (50g) plain (all-purpose) flour

4 egg whites

coffee syrup

½ cup (100g) firmly packed brown sugar

½ cup (125ml) water

2 teaspoons instant coffee granules

1 teaspoon cocoa powder

1 Preheat oven to 170°C/325°F. Grease 10 holes of a 12-hole (⅓-cup/80ml) muffin pan.

2 Combine sifted cocoa and sugar in a large bowl; stir in the boiling water, then chocolate, stirring until smooth. Stir in egg yolks, hazelnuts and flour until combined.

3 Beat egg whites in a small bowl with an electric mixer until soft peaks form. Fold egg whites into chocolate mixture, in two batches. Divide mixture into prepared pan holes. Bake for 15 minutes.

4 Meanwhile, make coffee syrup. Stand cakes in pan for 5 minutes before turning, top-side up, onto a wire rack. Serve cakes warm, drizzled with syrup.

coffee syrup Stir sugar and the water in a small saucepan over low heat until sugar dissolves; bring to the boil. Reduce heat; simmer, uncovered, without stirring, for 10 minutes or until syrup thickens. Stir in coffee and sifted cocoa; strain into a small heatproof jug.

prep + cook time 35 minutes **makes** 10

tip The cakes can be frozen for ready-made treats. Thaw at room temperature as required.

tips Fresh or frozen berries are suitable; if frozen berries are used they must be thawed before making the coulis. Ice-cream and coulis can be made 3 days ahead. Ice-cream will keep in the freezer for up to 3 months; the coulis can be frozen in ice-cube trays – this makes the coulis easy to portion.

vanilla tofu ice-cream with mango and berry coulis

¼ cup (30g) custard powder

3 cups (750ml) low-fat milk

½ cup (110g) caster (superfine) sugar

300g (9½ ounces) soft tofu

2 teaspoons vanilla extract

berry coulis

300g (9½ ounces) mixed berries

2 teaspoons icing (confectioners') sugar

mango coulis

1 medium mango (430g), chopped coarsely

2 tablespoons water

1 Blend custard powder with a little of the milk in a medium saucepan until smooth. Add remaining milk and sugar; cook, stirring, over medium-low heat, until custard boils and thickens. Remove from heat.

2 Blend or process tofu until smooth. Add tofu and extract to the custard; stir to combine. Cool to room temperature.

3 Transfer mixture to a 14cm x 21cm (5½-inch x 8½-inch) loaf pan. Cover tightly with foil; freeze for 3 hours or overnight.

4 Beat ice-cream in a large bowl with an electric mixer until smooth. Return to loaf pan, cover; freeze a further 3 hours or until firm. Repeat beating and freezing twice more. (Alternatively, churn the ice-cream in an ice-cream machine according to the manufacturer's instructions.)

5 Make berry and mango coulis.

6 Serve ice-cream with mango and berry coulis.

berry coulis Blend or process ingredients until smooth. Push mixture through a fine sieve over a small bowl; discard solids.

mango coulis Blend or process ingredients until smooth.

prep + cook time 40 minutes (+ cooling & freezing) **serves** 6

Swap the ice-cream
for low-fat yoghurt,
if you like.

tip To make this as a single large pie, spoon the fruit mixture into a shallow 1-litre (4-cup) ovenproof dish. Scrunch the four sheets of pastry over the fruit mixture.

apple and pear pies

2 medium apples (300g)

2 small pears (360g)

2 tablespoons lemon juice

⅓ cup (65g) finely chopped dried figs

2 tablespoons caster (superfine) sugar

1 teaspoon ground cinnamon

4 sheets fillo pastry

cooking-oil spray

1 tablespoon icing (confectioners') sugar

½ cup low-fat ice-cream

1 Preheat oven to 180°C/350°F.

2 Peel, core and thinly slice apples and pears. Combine fruit with juice, figs, caster sugar and cinnamon in a medium bowl. Divide fruit mixture into four shallow 1-cup (250ml) ovenproof dishes; cover with foil.

3 Bake for 10 minutes or until fruit starts to soften. Remove foil; top each dish with a scrunched sheet of pastry. Spray pastry with oil; bake for 30 minutes or until browned lightly.

4 Dust pies with sifted icing sugar; serve with ice-cream.

prep + cook time 55 minutes **serves** 4

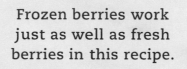

Frozen berries work just as well as fresh berries in this recipe.

vanilla panna cotta with berry compote

1 vanilla bean

⅔ cup (160ml) extra-light thickened (heavy) cream

2 tablespoons caster (superfine) sugar

1½ teaspoons powdered gelatine

⅓ cup (80ml) boiling water

½ cup (140g) skim-milk yoghurt

berry compote

1 cinnamon stick

1 cup (150g) frozen or fresh mixed berries

2 tablespoons caster (superfine) sugar

⅓ cup (80ml) boiling water

1 Scrape seeds from vanilla bean into a small saucepan; discard bean. Add cream and sugar to pan; cook, stirring, over low heat, for 5 minutes or until sugar dissolves and mixture is hot.
2 Sprinkle gelatine over the water in a small heatproof jug; stir until gelatine dissolves. Stir gelatine mixture into cream mixture; cool for 5 minutes.
3 Whisk yoghurt into cream mixture until smooth. Pour mixture into four ½-cup (125ml) moulds, cover loosely with plastic wrap; refrigerate 4 hours or overnight until set.
4 Meanwhile, make berry compote.
5 Just before serving, turn panna cottas onto serving plates. Serve compote with panna cotta.

berry compote Combine ingredients in a small bowl; stir until sugar dissolves. Cover; refrigerate until required. Discard the cinnamon stick from the compote before serving.

prep + cook time 40 minutes (+ refrigeration) **serves** 4

tip To remove panna cotta from moulds, run a flat-bladed knife around the edge to break the seal, then turn upside down and shake gently to release.

glossary

All-Bran a low-fat, high-fibre breakfast cereal based on wheat bran.

asian salad mix, baby also sold as asian salad mix and mixed baby asian greens; a packaged mix of baby buk choy, choy sum, gai lan and water spinach. Available from Asian food stores and most supermarkets.

bacon, shortcut a 'half rasher'; the streaky (belly), narrow portion of the rasher has been removed leaving the choice cut eye meat (fat end).

baking paper also parchment paper or baking parchment – silicone-coated paper that is primarily used for lining oven pans and trays so food won't stick, making removal, and cleaning, easy.

beans

borlotti also known as roman or pink beans. Interchangeable with pinto beans because of the similarity in appearance – both are pale pink or beige with dark red streaks.

broad also known as fava, windsor and horse beans; available dried, fresh, canned and frozen. Fresh and frozen forms should be peeled twice (discarding both the outer long green pod and the beige-green tough inner shell).

cannellini small white bean similar in appearance and flavour to great northern, navy and haricot beans – all of which can be substituted for the other. Available dried or canned.

kidney medium-sized red or white bean, slightly floury in texture yet sweet in flavour; sold dried or canned.

mexican-style are a mildly-spiced canned combination of kidney or pinto beans, capsicum and tomato.

sprouts also known as bean shoots; tender new growths of assorted beans and seeds germinated for consumption. The most readily available are mung bean, soya bean, alfalfa and snow pea sprouts.

white in this book, some recipes may simply call for 'white beans', a generic term we use for canned or dried cannellini, haricot, navy or great northern beans, all of which can be substituted for the other.

beetroot also known as red beets or beets.

blood orange a virtually seedless citrus fruit with blood-red rind and flesh; it has a sweet, non-acidic pulp and juice with slight strawberry or raspberry overtones. If you can't find them use navel oranges.

breadcrumbs

packaged fine-textured, crunchy, purchased white breadcrumbs.

stale one- or two-day-old bread made into crumbs by processing.

broccolini a cross between broccoli and chinese kale; milder and sweeter than broccoli. Each long stem is topped by a loose floret; from floret to stem, broccolini is completely edible.

buk choy also known as bok choy, pak choi, chinese white cabbage or chinese chard; has a fresh, mild mustard taste. Use both stems and leaves. Baby buk choy, also known as pak kat farang or shanghai bok choy, is smaller and more tender than buk choy.

burghul is made from whole wheat kernels, which are steamed, dried and toasted, before being cracked into several sizes, so they develop a rich, nutty flavour. Because it is already partially cooked, burghul only requires minimal cooking. Cracked wheat, on the other hand, is raw whole wheat.

buttermilk see milk.

butternut pumpkin (squash) a member of the gourd family. Butternut is pear-shaped with a golden skin and orange flesh.

capers grey-green buds of a warm climate shrub (usually Mediterranean); sold either dried and salted, or pickled in a vinegar brine. Baby capers are very small and have a fuller flavour. Rinse well before using.

capsicum also known as bell pepper or, simply, pepper.

carrots, baby also known as dutch carrots. Measuring about 5-8cm long, and sold in bunches with the leaves still attached. They have a slightly sweeter flavour than other carrots.

cheese

cheddar we used a low-fat variety with a fat content of not more than 7g per 100g.

cottage fresh, white, unripened curd cheese with a grainy consistency. We used a variety with a fat content of 2g fat per 100g.

cream commonly known as Philadelphia or Philly; we used a variety with a fat content of 21g fat per 100g.

mozzarella we used a variety with a fat content of 17.5g fat per 100g.

ricotta a sweet, moist cheese with a fat content of around 8.5g per 100g.

chicken

lovely legs trimmed, skinless chicken drumsticks.

tenderloin thin tender strip of meat lying just under the breast.

chickpeas also called garbanzos, hummus or channa.

chilli generally, the smaller the chilli, the hotter it is. Use rubber gloves when seeding and chopping fresh chillies as they can burn your skin. Removing seeds and membranes lessens the heat level.

cayenne pepper a long, thin-fleshed, extremely hot red chilli usually sold dried and ground.

flakes, dried crushed dried chillies.

jalapeño fairly hot green chillies, available bottled in brine, or fresh from specialty greengrocers.

long available both fresh and dried; a generic term used for any moderately hot, long (6cm-8cm), thin chilli.

red thai a small, hot, bright-red coloured chilli.

choy sum also known as pakaukeo or flowering cabbage, a member of the buk choy family; easy to identify with its long stems, light green leaves and yellow flowers. Is eaten, stems and all, steamed or stir-fried.

corella pear miniature dessert pear up to 10cm long.

coriander when fresh is also known as pak chee, cilantro or chinese parsley; bright-green-leafed herb with a pungent flavour. This herb almost always comes with its roots attached as both the stems and roots of coriander are used in cooking. Chop coriander roots and stems together to obtain the amount specified. Also available ground or as seeds; these should not be substituted for fresh coriander as the tastes are completely different.

cornflour (cornstarch) used as a thickening agent. Available as 100% maize (corn) and wheaten cornflour.

corn thins a thin crispbread made from corn; 97% fat free.

cream also known as pouring or pure cream; we used low-fat cream with a fat content of 18% per 100ml.

extra light thickened (heavy) a whipping cream containing a thickener. Minimum fat content 12.5% per 100ml.

light sour a thick commercially-cultured soured cream We used low-fat sour cream with 18.5% fat per 100g.

curly endive also known as frisée, a curly-leafed green vegetable, mainly used in salads.

custard powder instant powder mixture used to make pouring custard; similar to North American instant pudding mixes.

eggplant also known as aubergine. Ranging in size from tiny to very large, and in colour from pale-green to deep-purple. Can also be purchased char-grilled, packed in oil, in jars.

eggs some recipes in this book may call for raw or barely cooked eggs; exercise caution if there is a salmonella problem in your area. The risk is greater for those who are pregnant, elderly or very young, and those with impaired immune systems.

english muffin a round teacake made with yeast; often confused with crumpets. Sold in most supermarkets; split open and toast before eating.

firm white fish fillets blue eye, bream, flathead, swordfish, ling, whiting, jewfish, snapper or sea perch are all good choices. Check for small pieces of bone and use tweezers to remove them.

flour

plain a general all-purpose flour made from wheat. Also available as gluten-free from most supermarkets.

self-raising (rising) plain flour sifted with baking powder in the proportion of 1 cup flour to 2 teaspoons baking powder. Also available as gluten-free from most supermarkets.

wholemeal flour milled from whole wheat (bran, germ and endosperm).

gai lan also known as chinese broccoli, gai larn, kanah, gai lum, chinese broccoli and chinese kale; appreciated more for its stems than its coarse leaves.

gelatine we used powdered gelatine. It is also available in sheet form, known as leaf gelatine.

ginger, fresh, also known as green or root ginger; is the thick root of a tropical plant. Trim, removing any creases and knobbly pieces, then grate or slice thinly.

golden syrup a by-product of refined sugar cane; pure maple syrup or honey can be substituted.

hazelnuts also known as filberts.

horseradish cream a commercially prepared creamy paste made of grated horseradish, vinegar, oil and sugar.

jam rollettes also known as sponge rollettes; small sponge rolls filled with jam or jam and cream; generally purchased in packets of six.

kaffir lime leaves also known as bai magrood, sold fresh, dried or frozen; looks like two glossy dark green leaves joined end to end, forming a rounded hourglass shape. A strip of fresh lime peel may be substituted for each kaffir lime leaf.

kumara Polynesian name of an orange-fleshed sweet potato often confused with yam.

lebanese cucumber short, slender and thin-skinned. Probably the most popular variety because of its tender, edible skin, tiny, yielding seeds, and sweet, fresh and flavoursome taste.

lemon grass a tall, clumping, lemon-smelling and tasting, sharp-edged grass; the white lower part of each stem is used in cooking.

lentils (red, brown, yellow) dried pulses often identified by and named after their colour; also known as dhal.

lettuce

iceberg a heavy, firm, round lettuce with tightly packed leaves and a crisp texture.

oak leaf also known as feville de chenel; available in both red and green leaf varieties. Tender and mildly-flavoured with curly, floppy leaves.

marinara mix a mixture of chopped, uncooked seafood available from fish markets and the seafood section of larger supermarkets.

mayonnaise we used cholesterol-free low-fat mayonnaise having less than 3g fat per 100g.

mesclun a salad mix of assorted young lettuce and other green leaves, including baby spinach leaves, mizuna, curly endive.

milk

buttermilk originally the term given to the slightly sour liquid left after butter was churned from cream, today it is made similarly to yoghurt. Sold alongside fresh milk products in supermarkets; despite the implication of its name, it is low in fat (1.8g fat per 100ml).

low-fat has less than or equal to 1.5 g fat per 100ml and almost the same nutritional benefits as regular milk, with boosted calcium content.

no-fat see skim.

reduced-fat contains less than or equal to 2g fat per 100ml and may have extra protein and calcium added.

skim has less than or equal to 0.1g fat per 100ml. Sometimes milk solids may be added to optimise the taste (may also be labelled 'no-fat').

mirin a champagne-coloured Japanese cooking wine; made of glutinous rice and alcohol and used expressly for cooking. Should not be confused with sake.

mountain wraps a soft-textured, large thin, flat bread.

noodles

bean thread made from extruded mung bean paste; also known as cellophane or glass noodles because they are transparent when cooked. White in colour (not off-white like rice vermicelli), very delicate and fine; available dried in various-sized bundles. Soak before use.

rice noodles made with rice flour and water, a large variety of rice noodles are available, from thin to the thick broad flat noodles used in stir-fries.

rice vermicelli is similar to bean thread, only longer and made with rice flour instead of mung bean starch. Soak before using.

soba a Japanese noodle, similar in appearance to spaghetti, made from buckwheat flour.

onion

pickling also known as cocktail onions; these are brown baby onions.

purple shallot also known as asian shallot, pink shallot or homm. Thin-layered and intensely flavoured, they are used in throughout South-East Asia. They are available at Asian grocery stores.

shallot also called french shallots, golden shallots or eschalots; small, brown-skinned, elongated members of the onion family.

parsley, flat-leaf also known as continental or italian parsley.

pasta

pappardelle sometimes called lasagnette or mafalde. Flat, wide pasta ribbons sometimes having scalloped edges. Tagliatelle or fettuccine can be substituted.

linguine long, narrow pasta often thought of as a flat spaghetti.

index